A

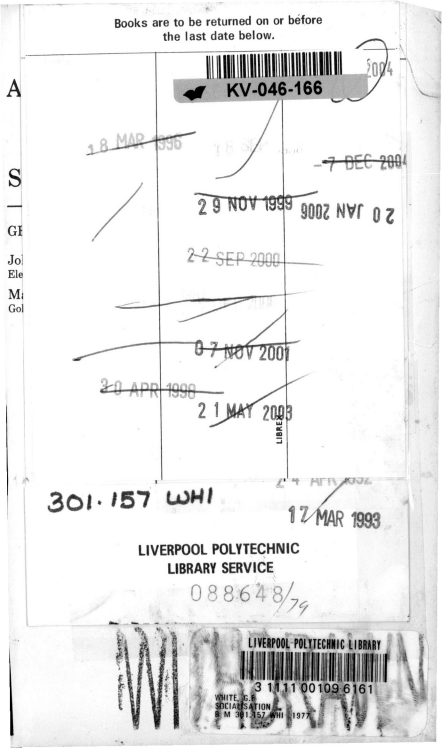

KV-046-166

1 8 MAR 1996

-7 DEC 2004

S

2 9 NOV 1999   2 0 JAN 2006

GF

2 2 SEP 2000

Jol
Ele

M.
Gol

0 7 NOV 2001

3 0 APR 1998

2 1 MAY 2003

2 4 APR

301·157 WHI

17 MAR 1993

For M'Elli and Jonathon

By the same author
The Character Training Industry (co-author), 1974

Socialisation

Graham White, M.A.

Lecturer in Sociology
University of Liverpool

Longman
London and New York

Longman Group Limited London

Associated companies, branches and representatives throughout the world

Published in the United States of America by Longman Inc., New York

© Longman Group Limited 1977

First published 1977

Library of Congress Cataloging in Publication Data

White, Graham E
  Socialisation.

  (Aspects of modern sociology; Social processes)
  Includes bibliographical references and index.
  1. Socialization.   I. Title.
HQ783.W5   1977   301.15′7   77–5792
ISBN 0–582–48532–0
ISBN 0–582–48533–9 pbk.

Printed in Great Britain by William Clowes & Sons, Limited
London, Beccles and Colchester

Contents

Editors' preface

The first series in Longman's *Aspects of Modern Sociology* library was concerned with the social structure of modern Britain, and was intended for students following professional and other courses in universities, polytechnics, colleges of education, and elsewhere in further and higher education, as well as for those members of a wider public wishing to pursue an interest in the nature and structure of British society.

A further series set out to examine the history, aims, techniques and limitations of social research; and this third series is concerned with a number of fundamental social processes. The presentation in each case is basically analytical, but each title will also seek to embody a particular viewpoint. It is hoped that these very relevant introductory texts will also prove to be of interest to a wider, lay readership as well as to students in higher education.

JOHN BARRON MAYS
MAURICE CRAFT

Foreword

My thanks are due to Professor John Barron Mays and Professor Maurice Craft for inviting me to contribute to their *Social Processes* series. Professor Mays has helped throughout in the preparation of this work and his criticisms have been invaluable. My debt to Professor Craft is much greater since it was he who, fifteen years ago, first introduced me to sociology as a field of study. Many of my colleagues have advised me at various stages of the book, and I especially appreciate the guidance given to me by Mary Farmer and Rashid Mufti though I am grateful to all who have helped. I am certain that they will instantly recognise their own contributions, and hope they will forgive the errors that remain, the responsibility for which remains mine alone.

To Barbara White who assisted in preparing the manuscript and to Margaret Grek who typed it all so impeccably, goes my heartfelt gratitude for making an otherwise tiresome task such a pleasure.

GRAHAM WHITE

The meaning and uses of socialisation

What is socialisation?

At birth the individual human being is virtually helpless. Ahead lies a long and complicated process of learning to live in society. This process is socialisation.

Socialisation is more than just formal education, for it includes the acquisition of attitudes and values, behaviours, habits and skills transmitted not only in school, but through the family, the peer group and the mass media. Moreover the contents of the various forms of socialisation are not mutually exclusive, nor are the agents of socialisation necessarily working in harmony, so the process actually experienced by the individual is exceedingly complex, and will vary markedly both within and between societies.

Parents are usually the most potent socialising force working on the individual in the early stages of childhood. Both consciously and unconsciously they push the child in certain directions disposing him to learn in a particular way. Powerful influences are brought to bear on the learning child by teachers, adult friends and neighbours, by peers and others. The physical environment, television and books all contribute in a haphazard way to the total learning situation. Although many socialising agents will share common goals they will not necessarily subject the learner to systematic influences. It is typical of our society that whilst there is often concurrence about broad objectives, as for example between teacher and parent, specific agreement about the means to achieve those ends is absent and apparently supportive socialising agents fail to reinforce one another. Similarly, each learner's experience is unique. There are no immutable laws which bind parents in bringing up their children, and the Jones boy will be socialised by his parents quite differently from the Smith boy next door, or his own sister, or even his brother. Parents will disagree about upbringing methods not only between the families, but within families.

Under continuous, if various, social pressure individuals learn to adapt their behaviours to conform to the rules and practices of the social group.

Such a commonsense view of socialisation neither derives from nor bears allegiance to any particular academic discipline. Rather, it consists of items likely to be discussed by young mothers at the local baby clinic or eager fathers at the bar after the P.T.A. meeting. Nevertheless, all the social sciences recognise at least the abstract notion of socialisation, embrace it within their particular theoretical contexts as a basic concept, and offer introductory summaries which closely resemble our commonsense definition.

Within the sociological tradition definitions are frequently couched in terms of transmitting the culture. Child (1943) wrote 'the process by which society moulds its offspring into the pattern prescribed by its culture is termed socialisation'.[1]

At about the same time Ogburn and Nimkoff (1940) were asserting that socialisation was the process which converted individuals into people.[2]

By the 1960s many writers were no less certain that socialisation was a one way process where the individual was the centre of attention. Elkin (1960) wrote: 'We may define socialisation as the process by which someone learns the way of a given society or social group so that he can function within it'.[3]

There were, however, signs that the view of socialisation as a die-stamping programme for producing suitable social beings was not a thoroughly acceptable model Chinoy (1961), for example, pointed out that the effect of socialisation was not in fact to produce individuals as carbon copies of their parents, but as active beings capable of innovating and bringing about changes in society.[4]

The clearest statement that there was a view of socialisation other than the heavily determinist one which stresses the conservative function of preserving society by fitting individuals precisely for social roles, came with the publication of an article by Denis Wrong (1961). In it he said

> socialisation may mean two quite distinct things; when they are confused an over-socialised view of man is the result. On the one hand socialisation means transmission of the culture, the particular culture of the society an individual enters at birth; on the other hand the term is used to mean the process of becoming human, in acquiring uniquely human attributes from interaction with others. All men are socialised in the latter sense but this does not mean that they have been *completely moulded* by the particular norms and values of their culture.[5]

Wrong's statement amounted to a penetrating criticism of the traditional sociological view of socialisation. Parsons (1955)[6] for example, whilst using the concept as a central analytical tool, treats it as an abstract and automatic process doing a straightforward moulding job on the individual: in his overall scheme of society a job of only peripheral importance. Nowhere in Parsons is there acknowledgement that as Wrong suggests, the individual is developing some unique attributes in interaction with others. Invoking Freud,[7] Parsons is concerned with the relationship between mother and child, and relates the socialisation concept to the development of the individual's personality, but this is regarded as the territory of the psychologist, and is anyway seen throughout as a control factor external to the individual child. The mother becomes a control agent operating within the family; a specific social institution enforcing conformity to its norms and values, in a situation where the child's natural instincts may often be in conflict with family and social norms. This social control aspect of socialisation is very important for many sociologists, and features prominently in studies of the family and education. Ultimately social control is achieved when self-control is mastered, and the individual is able to exercise discipline by himself over his own actions and behaviour.

Durkheim (1953)[8] suggested that the self-control element is not so much an adjunct of, nor response to a social control imposed externally, rather a moral order from within; an aspect of human nature. For Durkheim this moral order is so essentially a part of being human that it is immutable and incontrovertible, and so individuals display self-control because it is a component part of being social. Therefore being social is a moral and human necessity. Without society we would not be social, nor human, and socialisation would not exist. Society transcends the conscious being of the individual, its culture stems from generations of Man's association with other men, it is a social product, preserved and transmitted to individuals by society. From Durkheim's standpoint socialisation is concerned with the acquisition by the individual of basic social and moral rules.

It seems on the surface paradoxical therefore that culture, or civilisation in Durkheim's term, is an expression of 'co-operative Man' in association: even if this model of society is greater in sum than the total of individuals who comprise it, and society in every way transcends individuals, it can nevertheless only exist through them, and it is therefore inevitable that societal norms are internalised by individuals. No one is able to choose not to be socialised.

Internalisation of the contents of socialisation is illuminated by work in psychology and sociology. Freud for example has examined the development of social controls in children and with Durkheim has spawned a succession of studies illuminating the smooth progression from infancy to full socialisation. Precisely the sort of model which Parsons embraced and which Wrong has suggested conceives of man as over-socialised. This internalisation model is a static one, ignoring the possibility of conflict between the socialiser and learner being unresolved, or resolved in favour of the learner. There is no room for example for any possible socialising effect by child or mother, nor for contradiction between the needs of society and the activities of the individual.

Following the cautionary words of Wrong, it is no longer enough to focus on the malleability and passivity of the individual in the face of all powerful social influences. Without some idea about the individual's own activity in shaping his social experience our perspective of socialisation becomes distorted. Recently, research and discussion has been concerned with the establishment of models of socialisation laying stress on the techniques of the process, rather than the end products.

An alternative viewpoint

Sociologists working from within a symbolic interactionist perspective have captured considerable attention in recent years. In considering socialisation their observations have laid stress on the adaptation of the individual to the various social situations which he meets. The concept is still about fitting individual and society together, but the emphasis is on the individual's learning experience, and includes learning of behaviour appropriate to the various other individuals or groups encountered throughout life. The life-long nature of this model of socialisation is in contrast to the model from 'traditional' sociology which generally conceives of 'full socialisation' occurring at some unspecified time around the conclusion of formal education. There does exist work on adult socialisation from within this tradition, but this has never been part of a theoretical model of socialisation from birth to death. Life-long socialisation becomes a cumulative process whereby the individual is able to adapt existing knowledge and behaviour to new situations. A bank of social values, attitudes and actions is built up and the social actor can draw on these in combination to suit the needs of changing role situations.

This symbolic interactionist model of socialisation permits different individuals to attribute different meanings to a single social situation and represents another important theoretical shift away from the positivist tendency towards an over-socialised conception of man. Within this framework it is possible to see individuals developing particular views of their own socialising experience in marked contrast to another's view of an essentially similar process. These interpretations are in turn communicated to the next learning generation, to be interpreted individually once more, so a picture of immense variability is built up, comprising a vast array of 'normal' opinions, knowledge and behaviour. There are broadly similar features in all socialisation, for infinite variability would render the concept meaningless, but the notion of a range of normal socialisation allows for specific and highly personalised contributions to be made by individuals to their social situations.

Primary and secondary socialisation

It is apparent from this brief introduction that socialisation is a concept of great range. Some theorists have found it useful to divide socialisation into two parts representing stages in the process. Primary socialisation in traditional positivist sociology is more or less coextensive with socialisation for the primary group in the family setting, and concentrates particularly on pre-school children. On the other hand the symbolic interactionist would usually define primary socialisation as being concerned with childhood, and secondary socialisation as the process in adult life. As the positivist makes little reference to adult socialisation, the sociologist's traditional category for secondary socialisation is concerned with the phase of education at school and college, or socialisation for the secondary group.

These terminological differences should be borne in mind during discussion of family and school socialisation in later chapters.

Although the terms 'primary' socialisation and 'secondary' socialisation are widely used in sociology, any such division does not seem to add greatly to the concept. There is clearly a danger that primary socialisation is seen as a prerequisite for the secondary stage although this is not the case. Not only is it rarely suggested that one form of learning follows necessarily from another, but by some definitions of the traditional sort, both primary and secondary socialisation may take place at the same time. The practice of thus subdividing the concept is hazardous also in that lines of demarcation are not clearly drawn, and what may be socialisation in childhood for one writer may be the socialisation of adolescence or adulthood for another.

For the purpose of discussion in later chapters where subdivision of the concept is necessary, specific reference to areas of socialisation will be used, i.e. family socialisation, school socialisation, peer group socialisation and so on.

Sociologists working in the so-called primary phase have regarded it as a time when family and school enable the child to learn the values and behaviour to enable him to play his part in the primary and secondary group experiences. Much of the research has been about family upbringing and the influence of social class on the style of socialisation. More recently the contribution of the symbolic interactionist's work has been to draw attention to the development of the 'self'; a notion developed largely from Mead (1934)[9] which gives focus to the growing awareness of the child of himself as he experiences interaction with others.

Those working in the secondary phase have examined the broadening of individuals' horizons and the exploration of new areas of experience. Much of this work has dealt with schooling, and the 'problems' of adolescents in dealing with sex, drugs, new jobs and so on. It concentrates attention on the numerous groups which the individual encounters beyond the family and, especially for symbolic interactionists, after the school career is over. Study of this secondary stage of socialisation reveals the great array of social influences impinging upon the individual, and how as one experiences society more and more, the greater is the pull of fringe groups, and the greater the difficulties in reconciling pressures from different sources such as the stresses created for the working mother or father between the influences of home and those of the job situation.

In childhood, as in adulthood, socialisation concentrates on the learning of skills of attitude and behaviour, enabling the individual to exist harmoniously within social groups and to balance harmoniously the experiences between social groups to enable him to live his life with as little aggravation as possible yet keep abreast of the various role requirements of his life career.

Development of socialisation in sociology and psychology

The models of socialisation considered so far vary according to the emphasis which they place upon the importance of either the individual or society during the socialisation process. So the positivist sociology of America in the 1930s, 1940s and 1950s pursued a model of socialisation which stressed the role of society and culture in the relationship. Towards the other extreme, the symbolic interactionist concentrates on the part played by the individual in the process. Arguably the extremes of the continuum represent the main themes of the on-going debate about the comparative influences of genetics or environment over Man's behaviour. It is often assumed that the environmental end of the spectrum is the province of sociology, and the genetic end is the realm of psychology. Certainly the approaches of the symbolic interactionist are closely akin to the psychological view focusing on the individual's acquisition of the requirements of society, far closer indeed to that pursuit than to the sociologist's stress on the values and behaviour of certain social groups and how the individual becomes integrated into such groups.

It is an important feature of the concept of socialisation that it so easily transcends traditional subject boundaries, as in this instance between sociology and psychology. Indeed many empirical uses of the concept entirely reject any notion of separating socialisation into one or other subject perspective. This has been pointed out elsewhere [10] as being particularly true of studies in child socialisation and especially in the work of Bernstein.[11]

In spite of their often close relationship, it is possible to distinguish the sociological from the psychological aspect of socialisation. It is apparent even from the most cursory glance that many of the psychological studies are concerned with learning theory, whereas sociologists have considered the wider connections between family, school, other environmental influences and personality.

The use of the term socialisation appeared in sociology and psychology in a systematic way at about the same time. We have already noted a certain connection between the work of Durkheim and that of Freud, both of whom were addressing themselves to questions of the development of human nature in one form or another. In the early 1900s to 1930s Charles Cooley[12] in the field of sociology, and later George Mead[13] from a psychological position were contributing directly to an understanding of socialisation. Socialisation as a theoretical concept came to the fore in the early 1940s and began to appear in textbooks of both sociology and psychology. Clausen (1968)[14] maintains that the term in its present 1968 form originated in the late 1930s and early 1940s. This is probably a matter of opinion only since much of the work of Cooley and then Mead directly provoked subsequent discussion and use of the socialisation concept.[15] Danziger (1971),[16] however, supports Clausen and notes that both Park and Dollard independently used the term in the titles of papers in the *American Journal of Sociology* in 1939.[17] Danziger argues that the sudden upsurge of the use of the word socialisation indicated the existence of a strong force of supportive ideas. This would certainly appear to be true in the case of the psycho-analytic theory of that time. Isaacs (1933),[18] interpreting childhood behaviour in an English nursery; Kardiner (1939), and the anthropologist Linton, working on data from primitive societies and developing a theory of basic personality structure[19]; Newcomb and the Murphy's great reference work in 1937 actually using the word socialisation in the title to Part Two[20]; and most significantly Piaget's (1932) superb elucidation of many of the problems of socialisation gave the concept a great fillip in psychology during the 1930s. The cupboard was rather more bare in sociology, and it was not until the 1940s when Parsons (1942)[21] and the writers of the great textbooks like Ogburn and Nimkoff (1940)[22] and Davis (1948)[23], with the major exception of MacIver and Page (1949),[24] took up the theme that socialisation re-established itself in the sociological tradition. It is fair to say that the textbook writers, especially Davis, drew heavily from work on socialisation from within both psycho-analytic and experimental psychology traditions, and owed their sole sociological debt in this respect to Charles Cooley.

The connections between the sociological and the psychological views of socialisation are strongest in the works of the symbolic interactionists and particularly in the writing of George Mead, from whom so many modern ideas of socialisation have been drawn. Mead's (1934) work on the self has underlined the narrowness of looking at socialisation purely as the activity of social forces on the individual, and often unacknowledged, has been borrowed into quite recent writings on socialisation which regard the 'self concept' as central in importance. With all proper acknowledgement Davis asserts that the mainspring of socialisation is the appearance and growth of the self or ego. It is in terms of the self that personality emerges and the mind functions.[25]

It is worth exploring something of Mead's discussion of the development of self, since for many writers it expresses most clearly the notion of the individual in socialisation. The self has been defined as existing apart from the physiological organism; not present at birth but developing from among the interplay of social experiences. The development of self in this way indicates the existence of mind in the human organism.

For Mead, one of the essential qualities of the self is its reflexive ability: the ability to be self-conscious. This quality enables the individual to attempt to stand outside himself in order to see himself as others see him. The image so acquired then enables the individual to react to this imagined 'other person's' judgement. So the self is reflexive in that it can be both subject and object to itself.

The means of acquiring the self conception are those of communication in interaction with other persons. As we shall see later, much of this learning takes place in the family setting where parents are usually the most significant others with whom the child interacts. The child quickly learns that by influencing the feelings of his parents he is able to control in some part what happens to him. This process is summed up by Cooley (1902) in the most evocative way as the child's 'looking glass self'. Cooley suggests that it is easy to see this process going on.

> Studying the movements of others closely as they do [children] soon see a connection between their acts and changes in those movements; that is, they perceive their own influence or power over persons. The child appropriates the whole actions of his parents or nurse, over which he has some control, in quite the same way as he appropriates one of his own members as a play thing, and he will try to do things with this new possession, just as he will with his hand or his rattle.[26]

One important feature for Mead of this process is that the attitudes which the child seeks to understand and master can only be understood through *symbolic* communication; since these attitudes are themselves problems of meaning. Symbols are gradually absorbed by the child as he acquires the language of others. Once these symbols are internalised the child may imagine situations and responses in his own mind and judge how others will react to him and he to them. These imaginings will then be interpreted in action in reality. A child talking to himself, playing two parts, himself and possibly mother, lends startling accuracy and depth of meaning to the imagined part he acts out. By putting himself in the role of the other in relation to himself the child increasingly develops the ability to see himself as a social object.

This ability to objectify himself and take the other's part in his imagination permits the socialised individual to exist alone for long periods, although in essence man is solely a social being. The ability to live alone satisfactorily is evidenced by long periods of play as a child, accompanied only by the people and things of his imagination. More severely tested during prolonged solitary confinement in prisoner-of-war camps, this self awareness and imagination has often been placed as the main reason for the prisoner's continued sanity during such deprivation.[27]

The experience of solitude can only be borne after the individual has learned to take the role of the other, and can experience a form of social action within himself. Examples of children kept in solitary confinement since birth suggest that only the most rudimentary human traits exist without communication with others; although most cultural learning can take place rapidly upon the release of the child from solitude.[28]

It is not easy to say exactly when the child learns to take the imagined role of the other person, but in all probability most parents in our society would recognise behaviour in their offspring deliberately designed to provoke specific parental response by about twelve months old. Whilst still in the cradle, babies learn that imitation of mother provokes pleased reactions from her, and this is a very early stage of recognising the mutuality of satisfaction.

Mead expresses the reflexive character of the self in terms of the 'I' and the 'ME'. 'The "I" is the response of the individual to the attitudes of others; the "ME" is the organised set of attitudes of others which one himself assumes. The attitudes of the others constitute organised "ME", and one reacts to that as "I".' [29]

Both the 'I' and the 'ME' are aspects of the same self and it is not entirely clear always which behaviour should be attributed to which phase of self. Significantly the responses of the 'ME' seem entirely determined, whilst those of the 'I' omit spontaneity, or what Mead calls novelty, in the continual dynamic of the whole self.

In the search for clarity on this point Ronald Fletcher (1971)[30] contributes a useful summary. He points out that objectifying the self necessarily requires differentiation within the self. It involves 'the laying down of "memories", of stored "records" of the judgements, expectations, evaluations of others within particular social situations'. This 'objective picture of the "self", formulated by the reflection of "others" was the ME of which the immediate self-consciousness of the individual, was aware'. The 'I' being this immediate self-consciousness in everyday social action. Thus the 'ME' becomes the attitudes and expectations of others objectified to bear upon the actions of the 'I' and serve as the basis of social conformity.

Valuable as Mead's work has been for the development of the symbolic interactionist position, there are three broad areas which Mead's writing does not approach. As his is a model of cognitive development, it leaves out of account the emotive aspects of interpersonal relationships. Secondly his single notion of the generalised other is an oversimplification. As Meltzer (1967)[31] has argued there are likely to be a variety of others for each individual in different situations and at different levels of generality. Thirdly Mead offers no clue as to what is contained in the formation of self, he is concerned only with the process, and so no techniques which can be used for research purposes arise directly from his work.

Since the 1930s the path of sociology was distinctly towards a social engineering view, where social problems were thought able

13

to be solved by some socialising process upon the nation's children. Even today anxious parents wonder if they reprimand their infants too freely or show insufficient warmth, and worry about possible direct consequences. This popular view that children are conditioned by the actions of their parents towards them has been largely diminished by the efforts of Spock and more recently by writers and broadcasters like Proops and Rayner in the mass media.

This same historical trend occurs in the psychological studies of socialisation as well as in those of sociology. The work of Kardiner (1945),[32] for example, was largely designed around a social problems message, and concluded that to change society one must change the way one brings up the children. This focus on the production of socially desirable behaviour in children, of the clean cut all-American boy leads, not surprisingly, to a focus of attention on the major deviations from the ideal personality 'norm'; dependency on the one hand and aggression on the other. These 'weaknesses of character' were answered by psychologists by the attempt at the production of socialising experiences designed to combat such deficiencies. However, persistent research into the nature, history and repercussions of these forms of behaviour within psychology[33] obstinately refused to yield satisfactory definitions of these personality areas and only a few, unsatisfactory practical recommendations emerged. One result of this has been to concentrate laboratory research into narrow aspects of these traits, usually in terms of predicted responses to certain stimuli, but the distance of this work from social reality renders it intrinsically unappealing, and it seems to be saying nothing particularly revealing about social learning.

In psychology, as in sociology, attention moved from the effects of socialisation and the social engineering approach, towards the study of the process and the recognition that behind the action of the individual there did after all lie an actor, not just a pliable respondant.

Research in psychology in the field of socialisation had leaned heavily towards the analysis of learning. Considerable effort has been put into understanding parent and child interaction, and the way children learn from significant adult models. This move has included material from a number of distinguishable areas of behaviour, notably personality development, moral development and sex typing.[34]

Inadequate field data prompted many psychologists to concentrate their socialisation research in the laboratory. This represents a sharp deviation from sociology where empirical data relies on one participant in the process being both subject and observer. Although laboratory experiment may suit the psychologist's search for the details of, for example, the interactive situation involving mother and child, it is so obviously a false environment and subject to the experimenter's whim that it is unlikely to make more than peripheral contributions to a broad understanding of socialisation.

The quality and development of a field of study often depends entirely upon the quality and development of research in that area. In studying socialisation such research trends as have been evident in psychology imply a sad poverty of ideas if they depend for a subject upon the artificial experimental establishment of a social situation in the laboratory. We might hope at best that such an experimental theatre will stimulate psychologists to transfer their ideas into the real world. In the meantime sociologists view socialisation from a variety of different theoretical perspectives, but to their credit always root these views in reasonably true to life situations, and it is these sociological views that comprise the main themes of the discussions which follow.

Child socialisation: the family setting

Needs of society

Society requires that the individual should respond in appropriate ways to certain stimuli. Such a factor of basic stability is one of the most fundamental needs of any society. From this single premise it is plain that the socialisation process is closely related to a system of social control. In some respects it might be possible to conceive of socialisation as a pervasive yet covert mechanism designed to ensure cultural continuity, and social control as its more overt counterpart. Socialisation being concerned with attitudes, emotions and behaviour deals with the most basic categories of human social training. These are categories which, whilst fundamental, apply in the social training of adults as well as of children. ·

By way of the mechanisms of socialisation social control can operate. In childhood patterns of attitudes and action are established which suit the need for people to interact meaningfully and harmoniously. Later in life after some view of 'himself' has become well established, mechanisms of socialisation can still operate to dispose the individual to behave in appropriate ways, and to help him either to select the right attitudes and actions from his mental bank, or to learn new appropriate responses. This notion of oneself becomes enhanced throughout socialisation, and both in childhood and adulthood can become part of an overt social control system. For example, teachers will often appeal to what they suppose is an adolescent's self image by invoking standards of adult behaviour, or readiness to accept responsibility, when trying to coerce the young person into what may be considered a desired behaviour. The social control form in this respect attempts to appeal to the individual in terms of what he perceives as being behaviour worthy of himself.

The internalised controls which are established through socialisation, and the contribution of that process to basic traits of personality, ensure that individuals know in broad terms how to behave in any social situation, or at least have the necessary knowledge potential for behaviour. This does not mean that our socialised instinct, or conscience, is necessarily obeyed each time, nor even does this conscience provide the individual with the precise response form demanded by the particular social circumstances, only that what is plausible is available, and if acted upon will be acceptable. In this way broad parameters of social action and attitudes are established. These are usually satisfactory for controlling the individual's behaviour in society, though socialisation is more effective at social rather than societal prescription. This may be especially true in circumstances when the needs of society are unclear, or rapidly changing. Nevertheless the socialisation process plays a vital social control function and helps to ensure the reasonably smooth continuity of the society in which it operates.

If socialisation responds thus to the needs of society the question of who does the socialising is of considerable importance. It is likely that socialisation will be greatly affected by the individuals conducting it. To a degree therefore, it is in the interests of society for the aims and the process of socialisation to be overseen and regulated in some way. There is in western industrialised societies considerable investment by the State, by groups and individuals, in institutionalised socialisation in the form of education in school. Less institutionalisation is possible of family socialisation, and considerable variations both between and within societies are not surprising. It is largely through education and previous family experience that parents learn the appropriate ways to bring up their children, but society does not rely on this sort of hindsight, and powerful influences are brought to bear on young parents through the mass media, by teaching in antenatal clinics and readily available literature, all aimed at encouraging a sound basis of family socialisation.

The role of adult models

It is from parents that the child receives his first social training. Exceptionally children may not experience parental care, or any sort of small unit family life. For such children, socialisation is in many senses institutionalised. Whenever possible local authority care of children attempts to provide as 'normal' an upbringing as may be appropriate. Fostering and adoption provide in many ways the most satisfactory solutions, but where long-term hospitalisation in childhood, or some other form of residential institution is inevitable, great efforts are made to organise upbringing on some sort of small group or artificial family basis. Although this is common practice today in our own society, it is by no means the rule even in the western world, and indeed many young adults in this country born in the 1950s recall that their own childhood in Children's Homes meant rule-bound routines every day, a dearth of love and affection, and familial deprivation of the sharpest kind.

During the first years of life the child learns basic physical, mental and emotional responses and skills. Many psychologists agree with Freud that the essential personality is formed by the age of five. These vital prerequisites of social living are at the mercy of the vagaries of family life, and a broad spectrum of the child's future life style and opportunities are distinctly affected by the sort of family into which he is born.

Certain family and parental characteristics are regarded as favourable and others are regarded as unfavourable in terms of the child's opportunities to reach his developmental potential. To derive the optimum performance from the basic genetic clay

18

ink to having a further figure.
for Sex role.

probably depends upon the presence of appropriate social stimuli, though which stimuli may constitute 'appropriate' is much harder to isolate. Certainly emotional security is regarded as essential, and therefore consistent interaction patterns are looked for, and most studies suggest that apart from the basic requirements of adequate food, clothing and shelter, children need demonstrations of affection, opportunities to play, encouragement for verbal and physical exploration, and the stimulus of conversation and other symbolic communication with adults and peers.

Within the scope which such requirements produce, children are socialised to a greater or lesser extent. It is difficult to assess whether one form of socialising experience is more or less successful than another, and in what terms that relative success might be assessed. For the child growing up in a city centre environment, among the families of manual workers, a quick witted, humorous yet aggressive manner, with a free rein to be 'his own man' may, in many senses, be a more satisfactory socialisation than the experience of domestic elegance, carefully selected companions and the absence of the challenge of a physical dare. However intrinsically worthwhile that city experience may seem to be it is nevertheless likely to be the products of cosseted upbringing whose ultimate social experiences will make them the successful inheritors of high status. The individual child in the wealthy suburb may be better served imitating the behaviour and values of well-to-do adult models than is the city child in copying the mischievous bravado of his own age group. The models which the child sees, and which are therefore available to him to imitate, are very much the products of the social milieu into which he is born.   *link to Sex role*

Adult models are a crucial element in forming much of the child's early behaviour. The systematic and repeated expression of values by adults are learned and internalised by the child, and the first adult models, parents and other close family members, where the child feels physically and emotionally comfortable.

Such a rich learning environment encourages the child to imitate. The limits of that environment are set by the extent of the parents' own experience, so the more restricted the cultural milieu, for whatever reason, the narrower the limits within which the child may be socialised by parental example.

In situations where the value patterns and cultural experiences of parents closely match what is highly regarded by society at large, children will find it easy to associate their family life norms with the demands of wider social interaction. Transition from the immediate family setting to secondary group situations will in such cases generally mean no more than minor adjustments of behaviour, and will therefore be free of troubles and anxiety.

Where family and societal norms contrast, as illustrated for example in some of the classic studies of the relationship between values of home and school,[1] the child may well be faced with perplexing problems of choosing which set of values to follow in which circumstances. The consequent inconsistency of experience will inhibit the building of further socialising experiences and social development will be thus relatively retarded. Such a model is not simply a question of parents from certain cultural backgrounds being illustrated as insufficiently skilled in wider social graces to be able to create the proper learning environment for their children, but it demonstrates also that the child of a dynamic changing society requires to assimilate values and behaviour which were unknown when parents themselves were experiencing the socialising forces of their own childhood.

Arguments in favour of traditional teaching methods in primary schools suggest that greater parental support and therefore more successful learning for the child comes when parents find the school's methods familiar. When the hieroglyphics and strange jargon of the new mathematics are employed parents become bemused and as a result children are insufficiently grounded in the 'proper' learning style.

Some sociologists believe that it may be for the good of society as a whole if some individuals fail to fit sweetly into their social environment. The resulting conflict might ultimately be resolved in a change of circumstances which makes society a more suitable stage for playing out social roles. With this aim in mind the proponents of the conflict model of society would set their faces against any forces of amelioration. The Welfare State shores up the *status quo* in attempting to force some individuals to fit inappropriate social roles. This weakens the impact of the inherent social contradiction, and, in conflict terms, change for the better would only come about when any confrontation is resolved in favour of the individual. In practice, in our society, this is frequently not the outcome.

On the other hand, a consensus view of society suggests that the most valuable socialisation in the family setting is that which causes the least stress for the child when he encounters social situations in the wider society.

This is well demonstrated by Farmer (1969) who concludes that given adequate material comfort 'the children who thrive best are likely to be those who receive consistent parental love, encouragement and discipline. Erratic handling causes anxiety and insecurity'.[2] Alternatively, some forms of family socialisation can result in dire consequences for the child. Farmer continues

> material deprivation and emotional insecurity in combination are known to correlate with various kinds of social deviance, including delinquency. Maladjustment, too, is highly correlated with un-satisfactory homes and is manifested in symptoms such as withdrawal, retardation and aggression. Children showing such symptoms are frequently the products of homes where parents quarrel, where they are used as weapons in parental fights, and also where the parents are incessantly preoccupied with their own concerns or careers.[3]

It is increasingly the case that fathers play as great a part as mothers in the direct upbringing of children. Nevertheless it is still the mother who is likely to spend most time with the child and who is readily identified as the most significant socialising model for the young child. It is commonplace now to suppose that separation from the mother is the most serious form of experiential deprivation for the young child, especially if this should occur during the first five years or so of life, and our courts consistently award custody of children to the mother in cases of divorce and separation, even where the father's claim is by other standards the stronger.

Psychologists have continued to stress the essential nature of a satisfactory relationship between mother and child for family stability and the development of the child's personality. Although anthropologists can offer examples from other societies where children are brought up by someone other than mother, the significant stable adult model is always there.[4] This indicates that withdrawal of affection or inconsistent relationships with any adult figure acting as mother or father can create difficulties in socialisation. Recent attention drawn to the plight of single parent families has highlighted the need in our society for satisfactory socialisation to involve both parents with children in an harmonious family relationship.

The family setting provides a framework within which the child can respond to the systematic expression of values by adult models. On the whole similar values will be expressed by all adults with whom the child comes into contact in the immediate environment of the home. Value expression is systematic in that sense, and in the fact that those adult models will share views about the general upbringing fashion suitable for the child learner. As parents would readily acknowledge, it is not easy always to act and react systematically to one's offspring. It is easy to treat one child differently from another and it is even easy to be apparently arbitrary in one's dealings with a single child. Some transgression, for instance, may be smilingly reprimanded on one occasion and the same act elicit a rough word and a sharp smack at another time. The main difference

22

between the two occasions being probably something to do with circumstances quite separate from the child himself. It is popularly believed in Liverpool that children go to bed early on the Saturday evening after the favourite football team has suffered defeat, in order to avoid father's misplaced wrath.

When parents are the only adult models in the family, children receive the most direct, consistent and systematic form of family socialisation. Ideally, both parents play full roles in the process, although frequently mother's job is more dominant in child care. Father's role is, however, crucial, and any rejection of the child by father may well lead to just the same sort of emotional reaction in the child as any maternal deprivation. Criminological studies of juveniles often show delinquent boys to be afraid of their fathers, or otherwise rejected by them, in far higher proportion than for non-delinquent boys.[5]

In families where a number of adults other than parents are constantly guiding the child, some exceptional difficulties may occur. There are households where parents, grandparents, aunts, uncles and grown-up children all live under one roof. In such circumstances it may be that one adult, probably grandmother, assumes the main socialising role, but whether or not this is the case, any child subjected to such a proliferation of models cannot expect to get a totally consistent pattern of behavioural guidance. Indeed it is at quite an early stage that the child learns to play off one adult against another, so that in asking Mum if it is permitted to go and play in the garden of the boy next door, the request might well be prefaced by 'Dad says it's O.K. so can I . . .?' Nevertheless the more consistent and mutually reinforcing are the adult values transmitted to the child, the more systematic will that process ultimately be, and in all probability the more quickly will transmitted values be internalised. So variable are the 'normal' patterns of upbringing style in our society that it is unlikely that two adults will agree on the best way to bring up a child. Often variations are small and there is agreement about general aims, but it can often happen that fixed ideas will conflict, or that unclear views might be dogmatically asserted and clung to in the face of criticism.

Some pressures from outside the family

It is in this situation that the writers of the manuals on how to bring up the children can make their biggest impact.

Such publications are legion. Not only among the bookshops' best sellers, like the works of Dr Spock, but right down to hospital pamphlets and sizeable columns in the women's weekly and monthly magazines and even in the regional and national press. In the face of such bombardments, the advice, often contradictory, is bewildering. Young uncertain parents find their uncertainties heightened, their deepest anxieties unanswered. Modern society has no fixed pattern for socialising children, no rules are laid down, and such broad principles as do exist are not strictly adhered to. Indeed children destined for different social circumstances ideally merit different socialising patterns. Rather than specifying in detail the techniques of bringing up baby, advice is often restricted to passing on medical or physiological facts. When it does purport to be of a more social nature, guidance is largely expressed in terms of broad behavioural norms. So popular has the letter and column answer technique become that it is obvious that a great many adults are concerned with problems of socialisation. Unfortunately many letters elicit no clear answer. Advice columnists are increasingly coming to admit that they do not know what is the right amount of pocket money to give, or when children are old enough no longer to require a baby-sitter, though of course they would outline the legal limits regarding the latter point.[6]

Mindful of the teachings and the writings of many experts on child care, parents of young children strongly associate upbringing practices with the future personality of the child. Here again, careful scrutiny of the literature shows that many experts disagree, but the fact remains that the major thesis that child rearing patterns form personality, and especially that the first three to five years of life are crucial, has had a notable impact upon young parents during the last thirty years or so.

The era of Truby King brought physical exactitude for the child, and the sort of discipline admirably suited for the future public school pupil and defender of the Empire. The impact of such regimen is briefly summarised by Mary Farmer and Marten Shipman (1972) and the sigh of relief is almost audible as they write of the changes brought by Dr Spock and his firm faith that 'what good mothers and fathers intuitively feel like doing for their babies is best after all'.[7]

Many of the manuals on upbringing, and much of the direct instruction for parents on how to raise children are concerned with the administering of rewards and punishment. Most modern advice stresses discipline tempered with love and kindness. Few people would care to draw the line between acceptable punishment and unduly severe retribution. In reality the consequences of punishment are not constant and the attitudes of parents towards any misdemeanour are as important as the nature of the punishment itself. It is likely, however, that a warm, loving relationship between parent and child will transcend the immediate hostility of punishment, especially where patterns of punishment are seen by the child to be consistent, and clearly related to a transgression. The danger arises when the punishment is harsh and administered coldly or in temper and where rejection of one or both participants in the action is implied.

Trends in recent years have been towards a more tolerant style of child socialisation. As more young parents with reasonably good educational backgrounds embark upon raising children there is a complementary increase in the number of books read and advice sought on socialisation. Such advice is usually in the Spock mould, and as such is patient with the child, treating him as an infant with his own needs rather than simply as a miniature adult to be instructed. The decreasing influence of grandmother over the manner in which children are brought up may also make for a more tolerant and modern approach to child rearing. Inevitably there will still be differences across the country, and different sub-cultural groups and different geographical locations will respond to different traditions. However, regional differences may be broken down somewhat by instantaneous mass communication and the strong influences of education. Consequently there are likely to be more common patterns of socialisation existing in Britain today than on the continent of Europe or in America where a great many traditionally orientated commmunities still exist and exercise strong control over the values implicit in social learning. Indeed such influences have been so strong in America that only a few decades ago the puritanical values of family and communities towards the unmarried mother could result in the disposal or even the death of the child, and has given rise to the instances on record of the so-called wolf, or feral children.[8] These children were cited by writers on socialisation during the 1940s who were interested in the development of isolated children. Typical examples showed that children who had been isolated from birth, normally being kept in an upstairs locked room received only enough care just to keep them alive. These infants seldom moved. Their clothing and bedding was rudimentary and dirty and they remained in this situation almost totally devoid of other human contact for a period of five or six years. When released the children in these examples were unable to talk, walk or do anything that the normally intelligent child of five or six years old would be able to do. In spite of this apathetic emaciated condition these children were able to make up not only their biological deficiencies but particularly their social deficiences in a very short space of time, and during four or five years of accelerated socialisation they were able to learn to walk and even run, to understand language and use it in a rudimentary way, develop a sense of rhythm and in all other respects make the sort of progress typical in a normal child of two or three years old. These studies revealed to researchers at the time that the personality phases which they thought of as being basic to the human mind were not present unless placed there through communication with other people.

Even where society exercises a powerful constraint upon the ways of socialisation there are a number of features of family life which profoundly influence that process. It has already been suggested that love is important, and that children need the consistent experience of a stable home life with the involvement of both parents, and that a well balanced child grows in the home of psychologically and socially well balanced parents. All these factors are heavily stressed in the columns of the press, in books, on television and radio. Mother is a key variable, and her personality inevitably influences the manner in which the child grows. Size of family, material circumstances of the home and the sex of the child all have important parts to play in the child's career of social learning.

Social class variations

At one extreme a child may have a young, lively mother who is interesting at the sort of level which appeals to the child, who is well educated, confident in meeting people and prepared always to involve the child in her activities. This mother encourages a loving, sharing and comfortable family setting which brings together parents and children in a range of shared family activities. Mother will ensure that each day will present something new and exciting to do. The child will meet other children and when old enough will go to play school and mix with his age mates who also come from pleasant homes with charming parents. At home the child will have his own room, toys, opportunities to experience adventurous play in his own garden or in the park, always of course under the loving and watchful gaze of a caring mother. This sort of model beams at us from the pages of the women's magazines and television advertisements and is essentially a middle class family picture. At the other extreme is

27

an older-looking, be-curlered woman from a poor background; a mother with a large family who is tired of working, at least part of the time, at a job which takes her away from home. She is disillusioned with an economic state of affairs which gets her husband no work. She is irritable, anxious, particularly about money, constantly worried about the health of the family, and without either the time or the space at home to take a quiet hour or two on her own to relax. The young child is likely to be out of the house as often as he is in it, he may be brought up by other children, sometimes his brothers and sisters, often his playmates from other homes. He is likely to spend much time at play in the street until quite late at night. Such a child will certainly experience a pattern of socialisation quite different from the typical middle class child.

Although these models are at best the poles of a continuum, they serve to underline the apparent impact of social class upon children in the home.

Of the social variables influencing the socialising activity in the family, the variable with the greatest impact and the one which has had most attention paid to it is social class. Aims and activities of parents, the techniques of family socialisation adopted, the expectations for and of the child, and the specific training pattern to which he is subject are all likely to vary in such a way that in terms of the foregoing types the attitudes towards child socialisation are from the point of view of society more desirable within one social stratum than another.

As late as the nineteenth century the poorest and largest sections of the populations of Europe did not lead a family life as we know it today. From an early age children, especially boys, were separated from their parents to live and work amongst adults. The nobility, the rich merchants and craftsmen were able to live home life with their children, often on a grand scale with the whole network of family relations living and working together on the one estate. These homes were almost villages and provided virtually all the necessities of community life under the one roof. The basis of this life style persists in the modern, much smaller family unit, though now it has spread away from the upper and middle classes to include the working class, and so embrace the whole of society.

As the new pattern of family life spread throughout society, it took the place of old community based social relationships which had typified both rural and town life during the Middle Ages. Of necessity it took on many of the social functions which had hitherto been undertaken in the society at large, and education in the widest sense was the most important of these. With this change social relations became more focused, and the family more of a 'private' institution. Family activities came to revolve around the children, and socialisation of children in the family way of life became the first priority. Only later in childhood did socialisation take place in the wider society. This contraction to the family style we recognise today took place at different rates in different parts of the country. The middle classes with a better established smaller family tradition made the transition more quickly than did the working class family. Changes were more speedily accomplished in London and the Home Counties than in rural or industrial northern counties like Lancashire and Yorkshire.

Ultimately, and without always acknowledging the historical context, sociologists of the family differentiated between the family life styles of the middle class and of the working class. As the nobility declines the upper classes are usually becoming excluded from analysis. With such differentiation, allowing for sub-strata idiosyncracies within classes, the lines of demarcation between child socialisation style according to family social class were plainly drawn.

Unlike the newly formed small family of the nineteenth century, present-day families have a very clear idea of what they must do. Education and the mass media, the behavioural sciences of psychology and sociology in popular form have ensured that the standards of child socialisation are middle class, and deeply concerned with the emotional, physical, moral, sexual and social well-being of the child.

A considerable number of variations in the manner of child socialisation between the middle class and working class, together with speculations as to the possible effects of these differences have been noted by sociologists. The notion of class, being a generalised view of a range of occupations, values, incomes, educational levels, and so on, limits what can be said with authority about any single aspect of life within a class division. Similarly, forces which we have noted already as being related to patterns of socialisation, such as mother's personality or a happy and loving home, are not the province of one class more than another. So it is with acknowledgement to such limitations that the effects of social class upon the child's socialisation in the family setting should be seen.

Some of the earliest and most basic childhood experiences have been argued to be class related. There has been interesting controversy in recent decades on the matter of breast feeding. Certainly it was fashionable in the 1950s and 1960s for middle class mothers to use bottle feeds for babies. It allowed greater freedom for mother to work or go out and enjoy herself. Even the availability of cheap dried milk at child welfare clinics failed to encourage the working class mother to respond to the fashion with the same enthusiasm even when she did catch up with the literature expounding the virtues of the scientifically controlled dried milk diet.

The latest swing to the breast has meant that the middle class mothers, up with current trends and the clinic brochures, have reverted to breast feeding, passing the working class mother going the other way. It is very recent evidence which suggests that the working class mother has joined her middle class counterpart in giving baby her own milk, at least for the first few weeks of the child's life. Medical insistance that this is best for baby has underwritten the fashion and sinister statistics during 1976 which suggested a connection between bottle feeding and so-called cot deaths has further established the pattern.[9]

Further class differences in socialisation stem from these earliest examples of communication between mother and her child. As the child gets older he is likely to experience forms of reward and punishment in accordance with his class of origin. The model middle class mother exercises self-control in dealing with her child, no matter how extreme the circumstances, and such restraint is reflected not only in forms of punishment, but in reward as well. She makes great efforts to explain to her child the reasons for behaving or not behaving in a certain fashion, and wherever possible the exercise of discipline is within a clearly expressed framework of rationality. Punishments are designed to fit crimes, and rewards suit virtues. In order to scale actions in this way, the intentions of the actor, in this case the child, play a significant part in the middle class mother's socialising scheme. Windows broken by chance or by accident will merit more restrained correction for the child than any deliberate act. The working class mother in our ideal state will punish spontaneously and physically the act itself, not the intention behind it. As in other examples of life style the middle class tendency towards reasoned action creates a consistent atmosphere, whilst the working class pattern is much less consistent even in its physical violence.

At the other extreme the working class child may be grossly indulged with money, sweets and presents, and other privileges like being allowed to stay out late to play, or to watch late night television movies. Here again treatment is inconsistent, and such rewards may be extended or withdrawn arbitrarily.

Explanation for such behaviour on the part of the working class parent is rarely forthcoming. Such reasons as are offered for punishment are closely mother orientated. Children are rewarded by Mum as much out of her desire for self gratification as for any other reason. She may wish to demonstrate affection, or to receive a hug from the child. Punishment is distributed at her whim as well; if questioned her only reason is because she says

31

so, or simply because she is mother. There is no reference to the extrinsic factors or long term objectives so beloved of middle class parents when reasoning concurrence into their children. The verbal skills of the middle class also make it likely that the heat can be taken out of the confrontation by discussion and the working class manner of speedy physical intervention is rarely invoked.

If these patterns are in any respect true, and they are very much 'ideal type' positions, such socialisation should have clearly distinguishable effects upon the children of the two classes.

It can be argued that the verbal reasoning of the middle class and the love-related methods of reward and punishment which communicate praise and approval as a positive sanction or reward, and disapproval, disappointment and a sense of disloyalty as negative sanctions or punishments, breeds a sense of self-discipline in the child. Such responsibility is tempered with compassion for the feelings of others and in combination ensures a sensitive, law-abiding citizen, one who does not need the constant presence of authority in order to enable him to lead a full and honest life. This is the sort of person who can see immediate temptations or obstacles in a long-term context and strive to overcome them. A time scale which is anyway the privilege of the middle classes to enjoy since they have the means to achieve the long-term goals, and the resources to cushion them from the harsh realities of the sort of social experience which is the lot of our 'ideal type' of working class family.

Ultimately the socialising pressures of a particular sort are internalised by the individual and largely stamp his personality and the values and behaviour which he manifests. Although undeniably both working class and middle class families socialise their children within the framework of the same broad tradition, and want their children to be law-abiding, happy and successful, the perspectives on such requirements are likely to be quite different, as indeed are the opportunities for the children.

Farmer (1969) has argued that the attributes encouraged by

the middle class style of socialisation, including incidentally their passion for keeping pets, makes for adults with qualities of compassion and selflessness, combined with self-control and personal integrity highly suited for entry into the professions in law, accountancy, medicine and teaching; and for the years of training and self-denial prior to qualification.

Of the working class attributes Farmer stresses their respectability, cleanliness, tidiness and punctuality. The desire for obedience of the working class child is in order not to discredit the family and this emphasis 'is said to affect the subservient adult roles that many will be called upon to play later in the community and at work'.[10]

These two class positions are best seen as the poles of a continuum, and today it is likely that the process of 'embourgeoisement', the gradual merging of the working classes into the values and life-style of the middle class, is reducing these differences drastically. In that respect it is likely that the socialisation process experienced by the child of the manual worker will coincide in all but a few ways with that of the child of the bank manager or solicitor. Indeed it is quite common for sociologists to argue that socialising patterns differ more according to sex than according to social class. Certainly there are many ways in which treatment of girls and boys has been shown to be dissimilar.

Sex role socialisation

Socialisation into sex roles is one example of the forces of socialisation which impinge upon the learner's whole being, and by the time children are ready to enter school they are acting out their roles of boy and girl.[11] Imitation of mother and father, toys bought, types of play encouraged, and the patterns of sanction employed, push each child into the appropriate unambiguous sex identity. The learning of sex roles prepares the child for further interaction with others, and the early establishment of sex identity provides suitable conditions for further socialisation. This will take place for part of the time in school, where it is possible to identify sex-related behaviour which elicits different rewards or punishments according to the sex of the individual.[12] This view of socialisation implies the child is the positive recipient of the impact of social forces, whereas there are many examples in the family and in school of the child vigorously imposing his will on parents and playmates. Kohlberg (1967)[13] argues that the child's sexual attitudes are neither the reflection of cultural patterns nor of innate structures, rather they are the result of the child's individual structuring of his experiences of the world. They are not therefore just the passive internalisations of social training.

In simple labelling terms a boy is rewarded for doing boy-like things, and so he learns to want to be a boy, and behaves in socially approved boy fashion. The opposite is true for girls, and both roles are reinforced by powerful adult models. Although girls quickly learn that females are seen as less powerful and competent than men, the stereotype female adult is still powerfully attractive enough to appeal to girls.

In school there are plenty of play opportunities and girls and boys are not encouraged to play with the toys typically identified with the other sex and, partly as a result, friendship groups tend to be single sex. The influence of symbolic models, such as television, are strongly orientated towards the clarification of roles for boys and girls, and the literature in school may be a powerful influence in leading boys and girls to behave in particular ways. Critics of this trend in school books argue that it is a feature of sex discrimination when socialisation towards socially approved objectives has the latent function of being a divisive force.

Weitzman's (1972) researches in America examined books read by pre-school and infant school children, and concluded that women are characterised as being unimportant, passive and immobile. In all probability this encourages passivity in girls and may therefore work to their disadvantage since passive children perform relatively poorly in intellectual tests. By contrast boys are consistently seen as being brave and adventurous, with consequent social and intellectual advantages over girls.[14]

As children get older they are still exposed to the literary pressures to conform to traditional socially accepted sex stereotypes. Older girls aim at a model of the charming witty wife, the efficient home maker and warm mother, and may later feel depression as they find this ideal goal unobtainable. The stereotype is accentuated in magazine articles and television programmes and many women may experience a lowering of self-esteem in the face of their clear lack of success in living up to this ideal type. The narrow demarcation of sex roles in our society may also be harmful in that such restrictions offer women fulfilment only in the spheres of glamour and service. Although the ability to alternate role performance between men and women is becoming more fashionable in our society, much socialisation still received by children works against this trend. It is difficult to ignore the evidence which shows that what is learned in family and school is not easily unlearned, and that includes the clear distinction that men and women are different and unequal.[15]

The definitions that are established in our society support sex inequality. Many feminists would argue that this inequality cannot be supported by inherited differences alone. Anthropological studies of various societies do reveal variations to this pattern, but in most instances it is the boys who learn to be the leaders and the girls who learn to be led, and until our society becomes one where aggression and leadership diminish with the disappearance of competition, this state of affairs is likely to continue to hold true, notwithstanding any government legislation.

Interaction between mother and infant

Most of the discussion of family socialisation thus far has been within a framework of traditional sociology; a structural functional view of the family serving society in moulding its membership to fill certain general social requirements and various specific roles. In such a learning situation the child passively receives the models, instructions and styles which the family of origin purveys. Although much of what is entailed therein involves interaction, particularly between parent and child, it is nevertheless an interaction in which the child plays the part of the recipient, the learner, the clay to be modelled, the unformed individual to be moulded.

It is precisely that process of interaction which is the focus for the symbolic interactionist perspective of family socialisation. We have noted elsewhere that the child's interaction with his environment and the people therein can be thought of as creating an awareness of himself as a unique being with a mind of his own. This is a process which continues as the child gets older, and as the awareness of self is gradually built up.

The concentration of the symbolic interaction theorists upon this formation of the self inevitably focuses our attention upon certain aspects and various stages of childhood. It will be useful therefore to compare instances of this symbolic interaction view of the elements of child socialisation from within the more traditional framework of sociological theory.

In considering the newborn infant some discussion of the possible effects of breast or bottle feeding was offered, with reference to their supposed class relatedness. From the interactionist perspective the first signs of the infant's awareness of the mother are all important. From very early days the mother will become aware that the child has developed certain simple expectations of her, particularly in relation to feeding or cuddling or voice sounds. Similarly mother will expect certain reactions from the child, smile for smile, or perhaps reactions which only mother would recognize. Already a reciprocal pattern is established: both the child and mother reacting to, or being socialised by the other. As yet, however, the breast or bottle debate has not included a consideration of the extent of meaningful interaction between mother and child which either feeding form will encourage. Doubtless as the interactionist perspective becomes more established these views will be adopted by the clinics, the mass media and other advice sources, and discussions of mother and infant reciprocal learning at feeding time will be commonplace. Indeed recent thoughts about the western way of birth, brightly lit, noisy, violent, painful, anaesthetized, and, frequently nowadays, induced to suit the nine-to-five routine of the hospital, have been clear interactionist orientated efforts to understand the experience from the point of view of the baby. As a result some parents are choosing to have their babies in their own homes, quietly and at the baby's own convenience, with the help of no one but the midwife, in surroundings darkened to approximate to the environment which the baby is leaving. Immediately the child is born it goes naked and still joined umbilically to mother to be held and cuddled whilst the cries are quietened. These first moments of physical and vocal communication are thought by supporters of this method of birth to be crucial in creating a happy and loving relationship between parents and child.

Early vocal communication from the mewling child, and mother's words and noises are important facets of the interaction process of socialisation. The calm relaxed voice of mother soothes the child, responding audibly to the sounds which the child makes. The infant learns vocal responses and laughs and coos at certain stimuli in a regular way from a very early age, and reciprocally mother soon picks up the baby's own noises and repeats them back to the child. The adult too is being socialised.

As time goes by words come to replace the experimental sounds of the child, and again mother learns the child's words as readily as the child learns hers. The development of language is a key concept in the process of family socialisation from whatever established theoretical position. The influence of social class in this regard is believed to be vital and it is an area well researched and documented, and one to which we shall return later.

The traditionally orientated sociologist stresses the part played by language in the formation of the child's cognitive abilities, in his ability to get ahead in the business of knowledge acquisition at home, in the community, and especially at school.

The symbolic interactionist treats language as important because it is the way in which the child appropriates the world around him. He uses the meanings, and symbols from the adult world and they become so much part of him that he interprets himself and his environment through them. Indeed he has no choice but to accept the meanings of those adults around him. He has no alternative of his own. Those symbols and meanings give the child's world its reality. From a functional theoretical view it may explain why the child of the middle class has a view of the world which may be distinguished from that of the working class child. The language used is different, the symbols are different, the appropriated worlds therefore differ, the realities are different, the truth is different.

So through language, and other symbolic representations of his social world, the child learns first the behaviour of others, then how that behaviour and his own actions relate. Thus he comes to know himself. He can judge his own performance by the behaviour of others, he can modify his own behaviour accordingly, and even imitate the behaviour he perceives. At an early age the child copies the others in his life. At play the child will be mother or father, admonishing a teddy bear, or dressing up to go shopping. Later, at an age around two-and-a-half to three, imitation of specific activities connected with adult roles will be built into the child's role behaviour pattern. Serious matters of life rather than play. So he will insist upon privacy in the lavatory, he will help with drying the dishes, or he may sweep the stairs or carefully pour the milk on the morning cereal. All imitative forms of behaviour, but no longer just play. The range of the possibilities for behaviour and indeed the character and context of them will vary from child to child, family to family, class to class.

From a sociological viewpoint the family is the first and foremost agent of socialisation. A perspective endorsed from within any of the theoretical positions employed.

Child socialisation: school and beyond

The school setting

As geographically discrete communities became merged through faster communication and increasing populations, it became realistic to regard our society as being nationwide, as having, but for a few exceptions, a single culture. With the increase in social complexities, socialising experiences within the family setting were not sufficient to prepare the child for the day-to-day adult world.

The degree of privacy enjoyed by the modern western family is illustrated in the specific nature of the social experiences which the child is permitted. Not only is the family itself a particular social experience, but the child's other milieux are merely isolated glimpses of society at large. The play school and Sunday school, the local playground or play street, the park or the children's room in the library, are especially childish and scattered experiences. The child is still excluded from a great amount of adult life. Few dinner parties, bridge clubs, public houses, bingo halls or betting shops show children in leisure interaction with adults. It is even less likely that the child will enter the adult's world of work. Such specific inclusions or exclusions for the child mean that he cannot simply by observation and imitation learn anything approaching the range of behaviour required of him in playing adult roles. Certainly the family setting offers profound and lasting learning experiences, but some other form of socialisation is required in order to complete the fundamental process of learning to take one's place in society. Such an important process has to be organized; and it is organized through education.

Charged with this responsibility for thorough basic socialisation it becomes the job of those who work in education to instruct the learner systematically into the ways of the whole culture; without regard for the particular cultural experiences which the child brings with him to the school. For it is in school that formal socialisation through education takes place.

Because of the great value which our society places upon the educational experience, our attention is drawn to looking at some aspects of the child's career through school, the sorts of pressures which make schools the way they are, the job which teachers do and the effects of the peer group and home background on the performance of the child.

Impersonal as the education institution may appear to be in terms of the task to be achieved for society, it is an acutely personal and immediate experience for the individual child learner. Recognition of this individual experience readily permits analysis of education in terms of the perspectives employed by the symbolic interactionist, as well as from the longer established structural functionalist view. Indeed the interactive focus in education has never been denied in the application of sociological theory to the field of education, although actual study of the symbolic process of interaction is a more recent phenomenon. Stenhouse (1971) has commented that education is first and foremost concerned with inducting individuals into culture through their participation in a process of social interaction.[1] Invoking Parsons, Stenhouse sees education in functional terms, particularly as organized to service a particular need of society, but nevertheless does not ignore the impact of interaction in the education process and in the development of the individual's potential. The influence of psychology on educational thought has led educators to pay close attention to the necessity of viewing each pupil as an individual.

To balance out the needs of society against the appropriate respect for the individual learner and his abilities has long been the tightrope which teachers have had to walk. It is easy to say glibly that the task of education is to socialise the child into the culture, yet permit him expression of his individuality. It is undoubtedly difficult to achieve this in practice.

It is the *process* of socialisation through education which is important. As with the family experience, it is largely that social process which shapes the ultimate adult social product. For the purpose of the ensuing discussion the setting for the educational process will be assumed to be the school, although private tutoring still survives, and the reaches of further and higher education fit badly into the schooling model, and even the variety of schools themselves makes the inevitable generalisations hazardous.

The goals of education are closely bound up with ideas about fitting individuals into society, or permitting the person full self-expression of individuality. The goals will vary according to the school, and according to the individual commentator. They are not even necessarily represented by the views of the head teacher. So to indulge in a little generalising of our own we might summarise school goals in the following way: social selection, transmission of knowledge, inculcation of moral standards, and socialisation. There are other goals popularly cited and other functions explored, but these are the expressed goals around which most head teachers would group a summary of the aims of their school. The details, however, are likely also to vary. Something summarised as, for example, inculcation of moral standards, might mean a range of objectives including the establishment of self-discipline, or the appropriate standards of manners, dress or style for the particular school or social class. In all probability individual schools will have a great number of specific rules and values related to such general aims.

The most readily appreciated of the goals of schools and especially of education as a system, is that of social selection. This is a widely researched and well documented field of study and indeed that fact alone has contributed to the widely held view that education is primarily about social selection. Even research into the primary stages of schooling indicates the extent of this inbuilt goal.[2] Accordingly there is great pressure upon schools and those who work in them to see schooling along the lines of a social selection model. Recently some educational thinking has questioned this assumed major function for education,[3] and this together with studies into the real nature of selection through interpersonal contact[4] in school is building up an impression of uncertainty about the precise role of education, even among those who actually work in the schools.

Notwithstanding these trends the more traditional view of education as an agent of selection prevails. This is not surprising since a wealth of evidence and commonsense exists in support. Long before the 1944 Education Act pressures existed for equalizing the opportunities for all children to get an education suited to their needs. Such a theme expressed by Butler in the Act of 1944 as education appropriate to the age, aptitudes and abilities of pupils summed up the belief that given reasonable opportunities all the children could, through education, demonstrate their differences, in order that they would fit painlessly and properly into our stratified society.

As it transpired the 1944 Act demonstrably failed to give everyone a chance, and many studies have shown the imbalance in provision between the branches of the tripartite, or more realistically for there were few technical schools established, bipartite secondary education.[5] Neither was the profound influence of the primary school in selection ignored by sociologists and educationalists during the expansion of research which followed the Second World War.[6]

In more recent years the study of education, particularly by sociologists, has continued to emphasise the selection function, and this is a view of education held by people from a wide range of theoretical traditions, ideological stances and academic disciplines. As Banks (1973) observes 'it would seem indeed that the technical and economic level of a society sets limits in the variations in educational provision but does not operate at a strictly determinist level'.[7]

Rather less tenderly, a Marxist perspective was expressed thus: 'Educational institutions are mainly concerned, not with developing abilities, awareness and knowledge in human beings – but with selecting at successive stages a decreasing number of pupils or students for statuses increasingly higher in the hierarchy of occupations characteristic of capitalism.'[8]

The socialising function of education is conceptually separate from the selection function, but is nevertheless related though subordinate to it. Inevitably the job of fitting children to take their places in stratified adult society requires that different patterns of socialisation be transmitted to children appropriate to the stratum in which they will find themselves. So for example, an aspect of selection will be to make known to a group of secondary age children what range of occupations are available to them. This focusing is itself socialisation, and it is the tip of an iceberg which ensures that the child is properly suited in ability and attitude for filling a position on the occupational ladder.[9] These attitudes and ability are products of the socialisation function in education,[10] and a number of studies show that different social classes think in terms of different occupational areas for their children, and that schools reinforce these beliefs so that by school-leaving age boys and girls have been so thoroughly socialised that they view their job opportunities 'realistically'.[11]

This process operates both between schools, where secondary modern schools and grammar schools still exist side-by-side; where either exists alongside a comprehensive school; between State school and the private sector in education, for example the public school; and also within schools where streaming operates, even in many modern comprehensives. Studies of the influence of streaming have demonstrated that life differs qualitatively between streams[12] and that as lower streams take less interest in school values so various areas of life come to lie beyond their knowledge and understanding, including the means to accede to higher status jobs. Recently, a boy from Kirkby, near Liverpool, who was about to leave school at fifteen, wanted to know what he would need to obtain in order to study for O levels. Apart from having heard the expression, he had no other idea what an O level was.

It may be that pressures in school from streaming, or from home background, prevent certain children identifying with the teacher and school values. Arguably many children from lower class backgrounds are socialised into anti-school values. Possibly, as particularly American authors suggest, adolescent groups are so clearly cut off from adults, both in school and out, that in reaction they form their own standards and values.[13] Whatever the reasons, and in reality these forces seem to operate in combination, the outcome is that individuals look to their peers for consolidation and support. Socialisation from within the peer group is a powerful force, often standing in opposition to socialisation from the school, but occurring, at least in part, as a latent consequence of it. Such patterns of socialisation occur the more readily in situations where the school's social selective function is clearly defined. With these considerations in mind, it is not surprising from the functional perspective, that many teachers find themselves faced with a class full of uninterested or resentful young people, easily written-off as school failures, pupils who are seen as being only suited for the lower strata of adult occupations. The perspective of the symbolic interactionist may stress other features. School failure may mean the failure of the school, rather than the failure of the individual in school. A teacher facing the apathetic class may be unaware of his own shortcomings in this relationship, one where he feels threatened and insecure, where his knowledge and approach are inappropriate, and where his own socialised self-image prevents him from getting to the level of the pupils with whom he works.

Whatever the perspective chosen, the empirical situation is the same; there are particular socialisation forms for particular groups in school, and furthermore these are forms of socialisation apparently unrelated to educational principles, and far indeed from the principles of equality espoused by the Butler Act in 1944.

School organisation

By looking at education as goal directed and schools as being established to aim at the achievement of educational goals like selection, it is inevitable that some view of the school as an organisation emerges. This is a view not wholly appropriate to an analysis of schooling, having been borrowed as a model from industrial sociology, but it is useful to see that one aspect of school socialisation is to give children the experience of working in an impersonalised and formal setting, not unlike the kinds of settings which individuals will eventually find in the world of work. Certainly the first change for the child moving on from the socialising experiences of home and the immediate local community is that he is regarded in school in terms of his objective, or measured qualities rather than more personal or ascribed characteristics which influenced reaction to him at home. Nevertheless the more personalised attributes continue to have meaning at home and among peers, and viewing the school as an organisation accentuates the distinction between these informally based values, and those of the formal school structure. In the terminology of the students of industrial sociology, the distinction is like that existing between the formal and informal bureaucratic organisation.[14]

In this country, schools which are State controlled are run by the local education authority. Outside of the public sector, private education accounts for a fairly small percentage of the school age population.[15] In any event the power of the head teacher to decide what goes on in his school is ultimately undisputed,[16] and in State education, head teachers are appointed by the local authority education committee. Through this arrangement and the largely State controlled teacher training system, the Government, whilst exercising no direct control over schools, may in broad terms shape the socialisation forces to which children are subject in school. It has also been suggested that the curriculum, and even what constitutes knowledge itself is decided by the State.[17] That is still, however, a matter for debate, and there is no real consensus of opinion about the part played by the State in education, nor indeed are the goals and values in the schools themselves completely standardised.

If we look at other societies the relationship between formal education and the socialisation patterns required of the State are much more clear cut. In circumstances where families may not provide sufficient inculcation of desired values governments may limit parental powers and extend those of the education system. In Soviet Russia, for example, schools are used to indoctrinate students into the ways of the communist State and to ensure full recruitment for essential occupations.[18]

Descriptions of the kibbutzim in Israel also indicate that socialisation in the community has replaced many of the functions previously undertaken by the family.

Although it is easier to see a clear connection between the intentions of the State, the needs of society and the system of socialisation in education, it is not only in revolutionary or totalitarian States that this control is exercised. This pattern may be plainly seen in rapidly developing societies, and is even evident in well established western democratic societies such as our own. Durkheim expressed one role of the school as regulating the moral climate of the nation,[19] and this is clearly one aim which we might see modern British schooling still claiming to fulfil. Although Durkheim was talking about a centrally managed French State education system, offering much less school and teacher autonomy than in this country, the basic argument is relevant, and in recent years educationists in France have noted the pervasiveness of educational socialisation in creating moral norms and those which define good taste or aesthetic standards.[20]

In school the child meets, for the first time on a regular basis, adults whose relationship with him is bureaucratically defined and therefore restricted. In the early years of primary schooling there is considerable overlap between the roles of the teacher and parent, and the precise definition and control of the teacher's role is much more diffuse than in later years higher up the school. During the primary stage relationships between teacher and child are likely to be friendly and relatively informal. This offers security for the child who is familiar with this sort of adult role behaviour. Ultimately the teacher comes to modify this relationship to one calling for response on demand, or motivated by interest, rather than from any personal affection. The extent to which this move from personally based relationships to professional ones constitutes a betrayal to the child of his friendship, depends greatly on the skill of the teacher. At the end of the process the teacher is concerned much more with subject teaching than with relationships with the child and he is likely to be judged favourably or unfavourably by the child in terms of his competence to teach, which is the manifestation of his professional role, rather than for any personalised reason. The change in this process is heightened by the change from single teacher classrooms in the primary school to single teacher subject lessons at secondary level, and the short time available for interaction with an individual teacher underlines the universalistic, rather than personalised qualities of socialisation in later school life. By that stage the child has become familiar with the rudimentary forms of organised bureaucratic life.

Early days in school

Upon entering school for the first time at around the age of five the child meets a whole set of new constraints. He must adapt to fresh surroundings, new people, time-tabled work and play, and possibly a whole new range of behavioural expectations. Even though many children now have the opportunity to go to pre-school playgroups, or nursery schools, the actual entry into the infant classroom will still mean that the first task for each child will be to learn the ways of the school, and to strike up a relationship with the first teacher.

The establishment of a relationship with the teacher is a most important first step in the socialising process of the school; from the point of view of the child it will greatly influence how happy he is at school, how successful he becomes, and will largely shape the course of his future school career by orientating him, one way or the other, in the value system of the school. From the standpoint of the school this early relationship is important because it helps to indicate the way this particular child has been socialised by parents, and also what he is likely to derive from his school experience. This traditional functionalist view of the child's socialising interation with the school emphasises, amongst other things, that the child's assimilation into the school's way of life will be strongly influenced by his experience at home. Relationships with the first teacher are partly dependent upon the experience of relationships with parents, or with other adults which the child has had at home and in the community. At school, where the affective relationship between adult and child is minimised, the child more used to making 'legitimate' demands upon adults, rather than personal, spontaneous demands, will more readily learn the pupil role. The degree of ease of assimilation into the socialising process of the school, and therefore the way that process will subsequently react to the child will thus be powerfully influenced by the manner in which parents have prepared the child for school. Children who have received reasoned reward and punishment, forms of communication like those in school, and who have enjoyed the pre-school playgroup hours away from Mum, are going to fit into the demands of the infant classroom quite readily. The child who has experienced particularistic emotional relations with parents, even one who may have been treated in a consistent way and be otherwise happy and stable, may nevertheless, find his familiar experiences and patterns of communication quite unsuitable for use at school. These patterns are likely to be related to family social class, and, simply stated, the child of the middle class family will be better fitted for entry into the socialisation processes of the school than will the child of the working class family.

After a very short time at school children make friends with other children. They are attracted by similarities and tend to form friendships with others like themselves. This may mean that those who dislike school will band together, and those who see the teacher favourably will be friends with each other. At an early age these friendships are likely to be fluid and changing but as the teacher's perceptions of children become apparent the rank order in the classroom will become appreciated by the child and friendships may form according to those perceived positions. Those whom the teacher favours will go around together, and at the other extreme, those to whom she is hostile will be friends. Nash (1973) has argued that such ranking is related to social class, and we might assume that in most cases those who are ranked in a lowly position are those who have been ill-prepared for school, and who see the teacher's demands as foreign and unreasonable. Those, in fact, of working class origin. The traditional function orientated sociologist would make much of this connection, and point out first, the importance of the peer group in socialisation in schools, and secondly the way in which absorption into the peer group with the 'wrong' values in the school's terms will draw the child away from the interests which are the teacher's primary concern. This polarisation of peer relationships into two sub-cultural elements has been graphically illustrated by studies of secondary schools in Britain in the late 1960s.[21]

In that these conflicting pulls upon the child exist, even from the early days of schooling, part of the socialisation process of the school is for the child to learn to handle that conflict as best he can. Clearly, this conflict is going to be greater, even to a degree where it becomes intolerable and unmanageable, for the child from the working class family than for the child of middle class origin. After all, these class-related peer influences are not once and for all affairs, they continue outside the school, at home and in the neighbourhood, where typical working class patterns of immobility virtually consign a child to a particular neighbourhood milieu for all of his school life. In such cases peer influences, and even possibly family values, are clearly anti-school in nature, and consistent. On the other hand not only does school operate for just part of the day and part of the year, but teachers change from year to year and later lesson by lesson, and the influence of the school as a socialising agent is thereby much diminished in a situation of conflicting values.

Where socialisation at home contradicts that of school, many pupils find refuge and status in the peer group. Schools have a place for this informal organisation in the lower streams, and this contention has been graphically illustrated by some of the case studies of schools. After early conflict between home and school, if close home–school contact is not maintained, the child will be left by the disengaging forces of school to be a smoothly socialised failure or early leaver. Apathy and indifference will predominate in his attitudes towards life. Where there is only slight home and school contact it is likely that the family socialisation will dominate, and easy home-to-school continuity will be inhibited. Where continuity does occur this permits developing socialisation according to middle class values. In this reciprocal relationship it is clear that socialisation can be seen to be as much about the way in which social institutions like family and school view the developing person and perpetuate or manipulate social values, as it is about the individual's own learning of such accepted values and behaviour.

Some socialising agents appear to respond to a hierarchical view of society by allowing some individuals to continue developing their misplaced values. Such acceptance of these misplaced aspirations permits the social misfits to fall by the wayside. In this case it is the socialisation agents and the selection procedures which are inequitable, not the individuals.

So many of these patterns of relationship are left to chance that it might be argued that the notion of planned socialisation in school is inappropriate. However, most teachers in most schools are familiar with the commonplace arguments about the connection between school success and family social class and believe that this awareness enables them to overcome the bias which knowledge of the child's social class may otherwise create. Many schemes have been put into operation designed to combat this tendency, both in this country and abroad,[22] and it is today largely the research of the symbolic interaction orientated sociologist which exposes the problems inherent in the teacher-pupil relationship. The interactionist's focus upon the relationships which actually exist between child and teacher suggest that it is the teacher's analysis of, and reactions to the child which serve to dispose that child to succeed or fail. This may be as powerful an influence as social class of origin.[23] Further consideration of interpretive approaches to the understanding of education and the teacher–pupil relationship appears in Chapter 4.

Relationships in school

Interpersonal relationships are the key to the role of the school as a socialising agent. Relationships fall into two main categories, those existing between the teacher and pupils, and the peer relationships between pupils. We will look more closely at each of these in turn in order to appreciate some of the contributions made by the school to the whole socialisation process. In the terms of the organisation theorist teachers are expected to retain affective neutrality towards the children in their care. This is probably most difficult to achieve in the infant school where the needs of the very young child virtually demand a show of affection from the teacher. In these years the teacher must try to spread emotional warmth amongst all her pupils, often in a class of over thirty strong. As the child progresses up the school the ideal of affective neutrality is more fully realisable, and generally exists to such a degree that any display of favouritism on the part of the teacher is regarded as a serious contravention of the normative school code, and as such fails to fulfil the ideal model of socialising interaction required of the school.

The manner of the classroom relationship between teacher and pupil is frequently the result of a negotiated settlement. Pupils often have a fair degree of power in class, they are able totally to disrupt lessons if they so choose; conversely the teacher has little real power, and although he may resort to threats which he would be unable to carry out, he is best served if his authority, the personal aspect of power, is sufficient to enable him to carry the class along the path he wishes. Hostility between teacher and pupil is a great threat to the teacher, and is most likely when teacher and pupil values fail to coincide. In such situations where school ought to be the most powerful of socialising influences it may be that if the teacher fails to demonstrate great interpersonal skills, the opportunities for socialising the potentially disruptive child may be quite lost. This does not mean that socialisation does not take place in circumstances such as these, indeed there may be many unanticipated consequences of hostile relationships in school. These can be shown most clearly in the deprived areas of cities where a very high proportion of a school's population may be hostile to the professed values of the school and the teachers. Such mis-socialisation may cement a rift between certain urban communities and the values expressed by the so-called mainstream culture. Urban problems of socialisation have motivated many researchers and teachers involved in schemes like the Education Priority Area action research programme to make contact with parents and the local community in an attempt to bridge the apparent differences in values between school and neighbourhood. The degree of success of such schemes is, however, debatable.[24] A rather more radical theoretical view of positive discrimination might agree that efforts like the Education Priority scheme, ensure the continuance of educational advantage, and its concomitant disadvantage, in order to ensure greater power to the ruling class. Success in education, and later in occupations, is only offered to those who show a willingness to embrace the values expressed by the teachers and school. It would be those children who threaten the teacher's position by their refusal to accept his value premises who consign themselves to a pattern of socialisation for the loser in society. Such hostility will lead to failure following failure, and ultimate apathy, in a society geared to success following success.

Analysis of this sort assumes that the school is weaker in socialising the child than outside forces at home or among peers. In fact, it is usually very difficult to assess the relative weight of various socialising agents. A particular teacher, or school, will have different effects on different children, and at different stages in the school career. Socialisation in school may vary as much through the differences in schools themselves, as according to the intake. Some researchers argue that greater impact may be made upon the culturally disadvantaged than upon those more favourably endowed provided the school's efforts are properly directed.[25] This debate still centres around the relative impacts of agents of socialisation, and as the proponents of the Educational Priority Areas asserted, it is likely that the school will achieve an effect only when appropriate attention is paid to the values of the home.

In circumstances where such understanding is not forthcoming it may be more appropriate to conceive of socialisation in many urban schools as being for non-achievement, where the teacher is consistently unable to make the goals of the school have any appeal for the child.

The whole of the school's organisation is so geared that the bright, receptive child can succeed, not so much because of a superior intellect but because he responds to the stimuli of the school in an appropriate way, and has been prepared to give the correct cues to those with whom he interacts. Where the under-achieving child feels most comfortable, where his cues and responses fit, is likely to be in the peer group, and it is here that considerable positive socialisation impact will be made. Once established in the peer milieu it is unlikely that changing teachers or classes will persuade that child to embrace school orientated values, especially where they are clearly in opposition to the values of the peer group.

The attention of psychologists has been drawn towards the analysis of classroom interaction and the effects of different styles of interaction on socialisation. Some research has noted the beneficial impacts of a democratic leadership style adopted by teachers in gaining desirable responses from pupils.[26] The authoritarian pose is less successful. Inclusion of the child in the decision-making procedures which affect the day-to-day running of the school is likely to lead to consensus around the socialisa-tion aims of the classroom teacher.[27]

What emerges from the sum of these researches is that teachers do not adopt a classroom style in an arbitrary fashion. It is something which is closely bound up with personality and deep-rooted beliefs. As in any interactional situation the par-ticular qualities of the personalities which go to make up the group give that group a unique style. This is equally so in the school classroom. The interpersonal style of any one classroom is not the sole consequence of the teacher's approach, or her train-ing or probably of any conscious factor, it is a result of the reciprocal expectations of pupils and teachers alike, about their own, and each other's behaviour. The outcome is socialisation of both child and teacher.

It would be naive to conclude that socialisation in schools results solely from acting out reciprocal expectations. Indeed it makes more sense to see developing interpersonal attitudes and behaviours against the background of social influences upon the deep-rooted beliefs and presenting cultures, introduced into the school interaction situation. These would be the influences more typically studied by functional sociologists, those of school structure and organisation, the goals of the school system, the understanding of the teacher's role therein by both pupils and teachers, and all the influences brought by social class, family background and the teacher's own educational experiences.

Virtually throughout the processes of socialisation going on in the family setting and in school, the effect on the learner of association with children of his own age group has served to influence the pattern of social learning.

Peer group influences

From an early age, children learn the language and the ways of other children. Younger brothers and sisters adopt the mannerisms and behavioural style set by the slightly older child. At play in the garden, or in the street, or formally in playgroups or nursery schools, tiny children are encountering and adopting forms of verbal expression and learning how to relate to each other.

Up until about the age of two, children ostensibly playing together, in fact play in close proximity with each other, but do their own particular things. By the time that this independence ends the child has learned how to respond to the orders or requests or needs of the other children. Promptly taking up a play role if told to do so, quickly adopting behaviour appropriate to that role, able to revert to another skill in a moment, ready to console or care for a child who may be hurt or sad, and in a multiplicity of other respects responding to, and learning from, playmates of similar age, the child soon develops mastery of such social skills. At these early stages of playing together, activity is often supervised by an adult or an older child, to whom reference will frequently be made for a variety of reasons, for advice, comfort or participation, and so on, and who will thus effectively contribute to socialising in this peer group setting. In many respects the presence of the adult inhibits the learning which is most marked at this stage. The protection afforded by the adult in cases of fighting, of negotiating demands, of physical risks by trial and error, acts as a barrier to learning many essential skills of the age group. Nevertheless if adult protection is not present then contact with other little children will soon impart to the learner the necessary basic techniques of getting his own way, how to make contracts and co-operation with others, and the rudiments of aggression and defence. At such an early age each child is likely to express wishes and respond in turn to the wishes of siblings. Much later, after school age, hierarchies become established in the peer group, and the apparently informal co-operation comes to an end.

For most young people, more important than being well regarded by teachers in school, is the desire to be popular among peers. The evaluation of an individual by peers is of central concern to most schoolchildren and, indeed, to many adults. Different groups of peers will reward different things and individuals and groups will be drawn to each other accordingly. However, at certain ages there will be some attributes more commonly held in high regard than at other times. Among schoolboys prowess at sport is likely to confer a high status, and the good footballer may be 'cock of the walk' in a Liverpool working class suburb, whereas the elegant batsman or bowler in the 'Raffles' vein might be the hero among middle class boys of the Home Counties. Among girls a certain daring or tomboyishness will be highly thought of in certain circumstances, others may have as their champion the girl with the best looks, the prettiest clothes and the greatest skill in the application of make-up. This variety is further complicated by the possibility that the most highly regarded child is not necessarily sought after as a friend, although Hargreaves's (1968) interesting sociometric analysis would suggest otherwise.

Attendant upon peer group assessments and rankings are likely to be two broad areas of influence upon socialisation in relation to home and school. Those children ranked in a lowly way amongst peers, and who may be sensitive isolates for any reason, can experience low self-esteem which, if not compensated for by marked successes elsewhere according perhaps to school values, may well lead to persistent under-achievement due to under-valuation of self. This may occur most often where the value systems of peer groups and schools are opposed to one another. At the same time, high peer status in an anti-school value system is likely to result in failure according to school criteria, since, as Lacey (1970) has pointed out in the case of his character Badman, only the most serious transgressions in school are worthy of him, and only the severest school sanctions will satisfy Badman or the class as a whole.[28]

The inverse of this model is likely to operate where peer values and school values are in harmony. In such cases the high school achiever will be the top of the peer pool and the low self-esteem group member will be the under-achiever at school. The effects of social class may well exacerbate the tendencies, especially in the peer groups where anti-school values prevail, and where family does not provide a stable setting for the child, the peer group may serve to do so, thus increasing the pull of peer group values in the absence of ameliorating forces from a third source.

The power of the peer group will vary in many circumstances, but whether or not an individual child favours a wide circle of peer relationships or prefers the company of one or two, that child will become sensitised to the opinions of him which are held by individuals other than those in the immediate family setting, or of those adults in a formal relationship with him in school. In circumstances where the family or school has a weak hold over the child the peer group may be in a position effectively to dominate the socialisation which that child receives. As the pupil moves up the school and enters the adolescent phase it is likely that he will participate less in family activities. In this age group, from about twelve years old until about school-leaving age, pupils who rebel at school are at their most vehement.

Adolescent boys and girls who experience these sorts of pressures at home and at school are likely to find the peer group their main referent. The young people thus seeking peer group support constitute 'problems' of one sort or another, and they may find themselves drawn to friendship groups made up of other 'problem children'. It is in circumstances such as these that young people can easily be drawn into committing anti-social acts and become labelled delinquent. The combination of the adolescent's search for satisfactory identity, especially where home and school are not supportive, with the poor self-image which the 'problem child' learns to adopt increases the likelihood that such individuals will become socialised into deviant behaviour. Labelling theorists[29] argue that once the individual sees himself called deviant or delinquent, he will manifest behaviour in fulfilment of the expectations comprised in that label. This may more especially be true when no other satisfactory self-image is available. It is an indictment of both school and home socialisation if indeed the adolescent, and school-leaver, has to turn to the peer group as the sole situation in which to discover a meaningful self-identity, satisfactory status and interpersonal contact.

It is undoubtedly true that most young people seek and experience identity among their peers, and although this invariably involves some move away from parental values, since standing on one's own feet, and therefore apart from the family, is an indicator of adulthood in our society, it does not necessarily mean final divorce from the parental value system. The firm and reliable foundation of values and behaviour established in a child through socialisation at home and school serves to enable the adolescent to take what he wishes from the peer group and decide for himself behaviour to which he cannot subscribe. Ultimately, according to this model, responsibility for the adolescent's moral career is in the hands of the agents of early socialisation. It is rare for the transition to adulthood to be simple. Neither family nor school seems to know when it is best to relinquish their grip. Year after year as students graduate, garrulous parents, sipping sherry, talk over the heads of visibly squirming graduands, extolling the virtues of their offspring to bored professors. Few parents make the transition to adulthood easy.

Indeed, neither does the peer group make transition to adulthood straightforward. Socialisation among peers is largely into group values for their own sake, enabling the learner to be part of another social group, to make friends and enjoy a certain status based upon criteria other than those used at home or in school. There is a point in the socialising process where the individual is in limbo, where the main experience is of conflicting pressure. This experience is most clearly seen in later adolescence, at around school-leaving, in the search for jobs and adult status, where there is clearly little continuity between the socialising forces of home, school and peer group, and where none of these throw any light on the basic needs felt by the individual at that time; needs such as finding work of a satisfactory nature. To negotiate a tortuous path through these conflicting socialising pressures is difficult, and depends greatly on the individual's personality, and the effectiveness of primary socialisation. It is as easy to slip into isolation by, for example, not estimating accurately the responses of the peer group to some behaviour or other, as it may be to become socially deviant by too extreme a devotion to a peer group ethic. In the end it is the learner's future concept of himself which will assist his passage through those stormy waters. In that sense it is the style of the individual's anticipatory socialisation, again something which varies from family to family, school to school, social class to social class, which is crucial.

The selection function of the school

Whereas neither the peer group nor the family are socialising agents concerned primarily with allocating individual children to their future places in their occupational market place, the school's job is often seen in this light. Particularly in our society where selection takes place early in life, the schools have effectively channelled children into various categories of job expectation at the onset of secondary schooling. This is reflected in the 'reality' choices of schoolchildren at all levels when they consider the kinds of jobs they might obtain. Turner,[30] in making this point in relation to his model of sponsored social mobility, claims that where a contest system obtains then, typically, schoolchildren indulge in fantasy aspiration for jobs which they are quite unlikely to achieve.

In Britain, selective schools have quite distinctive social patterns. The development of comprehensive education in this country has at least changed the clarity of these differences. As our comprehensive system settles down and forms of selection appear within the schools themselves, so the patterns of socialisation continue. Where streaming exists in a comprehensive school so in essence does the tripartite system. The effect of this is for the working class child to get much of the same treatment as his elder brother received in the secondary modern school. Ultimately, that child will be confronted with a realistic job opportunity, congruent with the values and achievement he manifests at school. Not surprisingly, where family socialisation teaches that new opportunities are available in the new comprehensives, there will still be discontent when this does not appear to be the case.

At the other extreme, schooling in the private sector becomes more entrenched as many of the old Direct Grant schools become independent. Such schooling is designed for a quite different programme of socialisation. In Wilkinson's (1964) analysis the public schools are shown to perpetuate the main stream values of society. The tradition of education for the aristocracy became extended to the *nouveau riche* in the nineteenth century and was designed to train pupils for leadership at home and in the Empire. As the British Empire diminished so these goals became

61

adapted, though the adaptation was relatively painless, and the intention to preserve the *status quo* persisted.[31]

The tendency towards conservative socialisation in education is not confined to the public schools. It is arguably one of the main goals of all educational establishments to transmit a core culture. At its most enlightened, such socialisation also transmits the capacity to evaluate the values embodied in what is being taught but, all too often, as Bernstein (1969) has pointed out, this critical awareness is only encouraged at the top of the ladder of educational success; to those who fail in education is denied the capacity to evaluate their experiences in educational terms.[32]

These conservative forces in education are widespread, but they need not be inevitable, although surmounting such emphasis on preservation is, however, not proving easy. The Marxist analyst would see the forces for the preservation of the *status quo* as going deeper than simply the nature of the school's choice of social values to be transmitted. If education is a tool of the ruling elite in society, existing to perpetuate the exploitation of certain groups, one job of the school then becomes the socialisation of acceptance of the existing social formation in both advantaged and disadvantaged alike. One possible way around the power of schools in this regard is to do away with schools altogether, or at least drastically to change their form, so that the basis of socialisation outside the family is fundamentally altered. The move towards de-schooling has developed largely from the writing of Freire (1972)[33] and, more popularity, of Illich (1970)[34] and is well analysed elsewhere.[35]

Working generally from the premise of Marxist social theory, the writings of the de-schoolers argue that the schools socialise conformity in children by emphasising certain modes of coercion and compliance. Included among the qualities learned at school are subordination, dependence, conformity, competitiveness and fatalism. In ordering one's day-to-day life, the school encourages punctuality, response to bells and timetables, boredom, and in some cases alienation. Socialisation at school encourages the carrying over of these behavioural forces into adult life.

In contrast to this viewpoint the positivist analysis of schooling tends to focus on the style of value transmission rather than the substance of what is being transmitted, and research into conformity emphasises the modes of compliance effected through teachers' approaches such as coercion, threat, manipulation of sanctions, and so on.[36] The arguments of the de-schoolers are concerned much more with the philosophies which underpin such activities in school and these approaches are echoed in the deliberations of theorists writing from what has been termed the alternative paradigm, or the new sociology of education.[37]

The influence of social class: an alternative view of socialisation

Many discussions assume that the nature of socialisation processes and experiences vary according to social class influences. Successful socialisation, as measured by achievement in school, is distributed unevenly between the two major social class groups; those of the working class, who tend to underachieve and be less satisfactorily socialised, and those of the middle class who are successful educationally and who adopt the values and behaviour applauded by the main stream culture.

Much empirical research in the sociology of education during the 1950s and 1960s addressed itself to the problem of understanding the relationships between the child, the family, the school and a rewarding educational experience. One of the main conclusions of such research was that family values and attitudes can make or mar the opportunities for successful socialisation in school, and therefore high attainment. In some families, attitudes to education motivate the child to strive for success in school, a prerequisite of which is to accept the standards which the school sets. This makes the job of the school as a socialising agent much more straightforward than in circumstances where home influences lead the child to be apathetic in school or, at worst, openly hostile.

A glance at educational traditions in this country suggests it is hardly surprising that schools are geared-up for producing successful children of the middle-class. Before the turn of the century education offered the working classes only the most rudimentary educational experiences, secure in the belief that they were capable of achieving only the barest minimum in educational standards. The socialising processes available through schools were, therefore, suited only to this view of social class and potential.

As pressure mounted for equality of opportunity for all classes to succeed in education and be socialised for equal life-chances in adult society, the significant step of introducing education suited for all was completed with the 1944 Education Act. This so-called tripartite system designed to offer three kinds of education suited for three kinds of child, was based on the belief that children could be selected objectively at the age of eleven[1] for one of these educational tracks because it was believed that by eleven, ability and potential had already been genetically determined. It was largely in response to this assumption and to find out why some children made better use of their educational experiences than others that studies into social class and school achievement became established.[2]

It was found that schools roughly matched social class, and that family social privilege was a powerful predictor of educational success. This rather upset the established belief that the school was the most powerful socialising force, and that the role of the family in this regard was little more than rudimentary. Indeed it became clear that the role of the family was fundamental, in that the child's earliest experiences powerfully influence the way in which he ultimately responds to school, and even the nature of educational stimuli available to him, by indirectly determining the kind of school he will enter. Since success in school, and more especially success in the highest status school, is the avenue to occupational success, the influence of family social class on the child's life-chances was seen to be profound.

If the relationship between home and school is crucial in socialising the child, it is important to examine why and how this is the case. It is vital at the outset not to rule out of account the part played by genetic influences on the child's socialisation career. There are bound to be innate qualities which give certain children advantages over others. Nevertheless when these qualities are held constant in research, as far as it is possible to measure them, environmental factors are shown to produce different levels of attainment in different children.

The pattern of work in this field tended to hold constant as many factors as possible, whilst a single variable was studied in relation to the results observed. This method alone has its shortcomings since the possibility of conducting this procedure satisfactorily is open to question. Notwithstanding the criticism, this approach threw up some interesting findings. J.W.B. Douglas (1964) looking for causal environmental factors studied the influences of the home on the child's educational career. He used working class and middle class family characteristics to distinguish the children.[3] His evidence, supported by other studies,[4] showed that middle class children consistently had more opportunity to succeed in education than working class children with the same measured ability. In the grammar schools and others with a high reputation pursuing a special brand of socialising process, the children of the middle classes were grossly overrepresented. Recent figures showed that 59 per cent of grammar school vacancies, and 84 per cent of Direct Grant and independent school places, went to children from middle class homes even though such children comprised in all only 38 per cent of schoolchildren.[5]

Three major areas of background related to social class were treated as central in predicting the use which the child could make of his education. These were the characteristics of the home itself, the use of language, and the attitudes and values expressed by the parents. Each of these areas of focus equally significantly shaped the nature of the child's socialisation, first in the home, and subsequently at school and in adulthood.

The physical environment of the child's home, such as the type and repair of the house, the space available to the child, the number of siblings in the home, were all factors which the investigators treated as indicators of the relative wealth or poverty of the family. The effect of poverty on socialisation at school was reflected in the number of children from such homes who left school at the earliest opportunity. Conversely the effect of wealth was seen in those children attending the public schools or who otherwise received socialisation at school fitted for the life styles and living standards only available to the wealthy. Economic factors such as these cannot in themselves make for inadequate use of the socialising experiences of school, but the studies show that the child's receptivity to the values of the school is thereby greatly diminished. This receptiveness, otherwise called educability, was regarded in a Schools' Council Working Paper (1970) as being principally determined by the socio-cultural environment of the home.[6]

We can conclude that the socialisation received by the child in a poorly off, physically inadequate home at least starts the child at a disadvantage upon entry into school. Those home characteristics are commonly identified as working class. This so-called culture of poverty view[7] argues the perpetuation of the disadvantaged through the process of socialisation which they undergo.

The second of the major social class variables to be considered was that of language formation and usage. Language is an essential element in the process of socialisation and reflects in the most communicable form the individual's perception and structuring of his environmental experiences.

Bossio (1971) noted that poor home conditions and family instability coincided with a restricted language development, to the detriment of the child in school and later in the outside world.[8] This implies that the home socialisation of the working class child inevitably hinders him by restricting the use which he can make of subsequent socialising experiences.

Bernstein's model was of two ideal typical language structures, one restricted in conceptual range and the other elaborate, correlating with the working class on the one hand and the middle class on the other. According to Bernstein (1971) the difference between the language usage of the two social classes lies in the context from which the language springs, and resultant perceptions and conceptualisations which are consequently qualitatively different.[9]

Language acquisition in the terms of this model produces two discrete processes of socialisation. The code of the working class deals with meanings which are context specific, its users employ emotive terminology and concrete symbolism, the content being generally descriptive and with limited phraseology. This stereotyped 'public' language resorts to changes of tone and volume for emphasis which, together with widespread use of supportive gesture, makes it a strident communication form, liable to outbursts of physical activity in support of a point, or where language fails. In so far as this ideal type of language socialisation really operates it is poor preparation for schooling. Middle class language on the other hand is the language of education. It entails socialisation of the child into the abstract nuances of high moral codes, it encourages self-discipline by its reference to universalistic meanings which transcend immediate social contexts and therefore offers the child a flexible basis for future action. Language acquisition becomes the means of transmission of subtlety of feeling and meaning, and the finesse involved in juxtaposing certain words and phrasing echoes this sensitivity of conceptualisation and perception.

These two modes of language socialisation differ in the quality of life presented and, in this sense, the working class are deprived. In recent years the notion of deprivation has been contested [10] and Bernstein argues now that the working classes are not linguistically deprived.[11] Nevertheless, in the terms of the child's socialisation pattern, Bernstein (1969) sums up the crux of the issue as a problem which can be understood as a confrontation between the schools' universalistic orders of meaning and the particularistic ones of the child's presenting culture.[12]

It is the relationship between the agents of socialisation which determine the extent of the success of socialising experiences, and an analysis of language in the terms adopted by both Bossio and Bernstein shows the working classes to be greatly hindered by the lack of any congruence between their socialisation process in the family and that of the school. The middle classes have the considerable advantage of a smooth transition between the values amongst the family and those espoused by the school.

The third of the three major social class variables is closely related to much of what has been included under the previous two headings and in many ways is all pervasive in any discussion of the relationship between social class and the process of socialisation. Encompassed in this variable is the belief that as well as physical differences, there exist discernible differences of emotional and cultural environment between the working class and middle class. That is to say all the attitudes, values and behaviour of the child and his family. A summary of some of these and how they might differ between the social class groups serves to illustrate not only the forms in which researchers have presented their analyses of these fields but also the kinds of special circumstances which are first-hand experiences for the child being socialised.

In an earlier discussion we noted that there are differences of maternal style between the working class and middle class mother. In terms of family socialisation as preparation for education, the middle class mother is much more likely to involve herself in the child's education than is the mother of the working class family. The role of the father is distinctive too since in working class families father rarely involves himself in the child's formal schooling. Maternal efficiency in pre-school socialisation is often regarded as the major single factor affecting the child's performance in school.[13]

Another important element in family socialisation for school is the way in which the school is regarded by members of the family, especially by the mother, and the extent to which the goals and values of the family coincide with those of the school.

Different social classes have different expectations of their children in school, these are reflected in different goals for the child and are therefore subject to different patterns of motivation.

Where the family places a high value upon education for its own sake, the child would be motivated to achieve the standards set by the school. Parental encouragement would provide continuing stimulus to this motivation.[14] Among the working classes this sort of stimulus and motivation was shown to be relatively lacking, indeed in some families parents were hostile towards school and despised teachers who adopted the middle class values of the school, especially when they had themselves sprung from the roots of a working class community.

Any lack of parental support for the education of the child may reflect the level of schooling reached by parents. Many middle class parents, with a high educational standard behind them are in a better position to understand school subjects and the needs of the child in school than are working class parents with a lower educational standard. At least they think they are, and communicate with schools in an uninhibited way, whereas the low self-image of the working class mother in relation to the school manifests itself in apathy or hostility; neither of which qualities assists the child to adapt to the values of the school. The figures given by Crowther (1960) support the view that the length of parental education is an important variable in the success of the child in school.[15]

Where lower class children have overcome the pressures in school and have succeeded in achieving access to the top streams, they have usually received a form of socialisation at home which does not conform to the usual working class pattern. They will have received strong parental support and encouragement and will not have had to plan to leave school at the first opportunity. This may occur when one parent has had a middle class upbringing or where middle class aspirations in the family are strong, and socialisation in the family according to middle class values is pursued.[16] Differences in patterns of socialisation between the social class groups may be exemplified through the concept of deferred gratification.[17] Use of this concept again serves to show the disadvantages accruing to the child of the working class family because of the values and attitudes which he is socialised to adopt. Rather than defer pleasure for the promise of greater delights, which is the middle class approach, working class families according to this model are traditionally orientated towards immediate satisfaction and a fatalistic attitude to life. Education, in that it imposes restrictions upon the child, and is based upon present hardship for the opportunity of future reward, is alien to the working class. If this pattern is true, it is a realistic working class appraisal since the jobs into which children of working class families tend to go are not demanding of high educational qualifications. This amounts almost to a tautology, but the low motivation to learn in school, realistically as it may be based on the working class life-style, is adequate socialisation only for future unemployment, low standards of living at home, alienation and despair.

Evasion of school becomes a goal in itself and socialisation according to these negative educational values manifests itself first in lateness and absence from school, then later in truancy and a form of educational retardation which becomes impossible to recover. In essence this third variable is pointing up fundamental differences in socialising patterns between the two major social classes which make for different capacities to use beneficially subsequent socialising experiences. Furthermore the suggestion is that the values, attitudes and behaviour of the working class constitute an inferior process of socialisation. This notion underpins the concept of cultural deprivation, the suggestion of positive discrimination, the recommendations of Plowden and all the paraphernalia of the various Education Priority Area action research projects and their subsequent programmes.[18]

The report of the Plowden Committee (1967) having indicated the connection between parental encouragement and success in education, pointed out that children receiving least parental support moved into poorly provided schools, frequently drab and lacking in amenities, and often with lowly-qualified and un-caring teachers. In attempting to redress the imbalance between this sort of experience and that received by the middle classes the programmes of positive discrimination planned to stimulate the learning environments of the most disadvantaged children by injections of money and manpower. Nevertheless, the impact of parents upon socialisation was still believed to be paramount and Midwinter (1972)[19] claimed that the first focus of the school should be to change attitudes towards education, and con-siderable efforts were made to involve parents in schools.[20]

In spite of the good intentions and the large sums of money spent, the education priority programmes have not been a notable success. In terms of the socialisation process experienced by the so-called culturally deprived children, little has changed. It is hardly surprising when the effect of the home during the primary stages of socialisation appears to be so powerful that tinkering with the system of secondary socialisation has little effect. As we have seen, socialisation is so complex that changes in education alone cannot, in the short term at least, generate the sort of changes needed to modify the whole process. Unless there are drastic changes in the patterns of opportunity for entry into the occupational structure then those children who have been socialised in conditions of poverty, bad housing and adult unemployment, even when parental hostility to education is diminished, will suffer in comparison with their middle class contemporaries. Nevertheless, the awareness of the disadvantage related to social class, and the attempt at compensation are a start. Now other programmes of social reform are needed to take these socialising opportunities further.[21]

In recent years there has arisen a number of criticisms of the methods used by researchers studying social class influences upon the educational and life chances of the child.

As we have already commented, defining all the variables in a given situation, then choosing one and holding all others constant, is virtually impossible. Add to that the methods of data collection which permit the value judgements of the researchers to go unchallenged and what we have at the end is not the scientifically neutral data claimed. Virtually any variable chosen, given the right treatment, will show a connection with social class. Preconceptions about the field are very powerful and even Plowden and other Government sponsored projects have been criticised for their pursuit of an administratively preconceived point.[22]

The notion of cultural deprivation, of a working class socialising experience qualitatively inferior to that of the middle class, has also received recent criticism.

Nell Keddie (1973) argues that since it is impossible for any group to be deprived of its own culture, there must be some view which marks as morally correct the dominant cultural tradition. She continues that the term cultural deprivation becomes 'a euphemism for saying that working class and ethnic groups have cultures which are at least dissonant with, if not inferior to, the "mainstream" culture of society at large'.[23] What many researchers into social class and achievement seem to be saying is that the dominant culture into which children *should* be socialised is that legitimised only by its position of economic and political power and not by anything intrinsically worthwhile. The idea of cultural deprivation refers only to those who cannot achieve the standard of fundamental socialised characteristics of successful children and it is therefore a term used to divert attention from a political and economic reality which purposefully discriminates against certain sections of the community.

In the comments of the de-schoolers many aspects of traditional schooling are questioned. The kind of research which concentrated upon social class characteristics and socialisation developed theories which stressed the failure of individuals and families in the socialising process. Bernstein[24] (1969) has criticised this because the school context is left unquestioned.

Indeed even Plowden saw the school as guiding and supplementing inadequate home circumstances. The critics concluded that rather than not responding adequately to socialising stimuli, the working class child was being alienated.[25] He was being bombarded by a culture which was foreign to him, pressing him to conform by using encouragement and sanctions which carry little weight in his experience, yet rejecting as inappropriate the attitudes, values and behaviour, which had been socialised into him and which he brought as his presenting culture to school.

One Marxist viewpoint on this is clear. Schools form part of a socialising process attempting to ensure conformity to an ideology which serves to deflect attention from the reality of the exploitation practised by the dominant classes. It therefore avoids confronting the need for fundamental social change. What is needed is that the school context, and the political and economic structure of society, should become the new areas for concern in considering the opportunities for socialisation made available for different groups of children.

Such questions take us away more and more from the traditional positivist view of socialisation in general and of education in particular. Recent developments have focused attention on the school, and the nature of knowledge, from an interaction perspective. This approach regards Man's social situation as a product of his interaction with other men, in other words an individual in a state of constant action with and within his environment, and whose values, attitudes and behaviour must be actively interpreted and not simply taken for granted.

Working from within the interpretive paradigm, as this focus has been called,[26] theorists in the sociology of education have argued that education itself may contribute to creating undersocialised children through schools and curricula. Taken at its most straightforward, this line of analysis argues that the school can influence a child, not only by the formal transmission of values, but by hitherto unquestioned practices as, for example, the availability for certain children in certain streams to sit examinations which, after all, are major criteria for evaluating school achievements. Ultimately educational achievement is the result of a form of socialisation experience in school determined by those who decide what constitutes achievement and who can back this decision by controlling school structures and examinations.[27]

How then are children chosen for the special socialising process which maximises their opportunities for success? Until recently the eleven-plus examination was the key selection procedure, though its claim to evaluate children objectively was long since shattered, and its failure to account for social class background effects exposed it to severe criticism. With the growth of comprehensive schooling, much more acknowledged reliance has been placed upon teachers' evaluations, what Simon called in a now famous phrase 'that inexpert rough justice'.[28] Because of this, the teachers' part in the process of socialisation becomes a key question for attention. Why is it that from the perspective of the interpretive paradigm it is reasonable to conclude that it is teachers who have limited the socialisation of lower class children to a basic form and who have enhanced the opportunities available to children from middle class families by their positive bias by reinforcing the tradition of socialisation in which such children have developed?

From first encounter with a pupil every teacher has some knowledge of a child's background, both out of school and particularly in school as the pupil proceeds through the educational system. The judgement of a child's needs is carried out by a teacher according to the facts and opinions at his disposal and then analysed, not objectively for this is impossible, but according to a number of idiosyncratic variables possibly including the teacher's own values and attitudes, social class background, his school experience, his position in school and his teacher training experience.

Teacher training, for example, embodies middle class values and it is during training that the teacher develops a strong image of what constitutes an ideal pupil, often by being expected himself to conform to school-type situations in college. The attitudes and behaviour of this ideal pupil model are closely correlated with high achievement. The teacher sums up children according to his ideal model and such perceptions based upon the child's general qualities like language use, personal appearance, values, self-image and response to authority, impute academic success without reference to previous academic records. In interaction, the view which the teacher has of the child profoundly influences that child's response and performance. Nash (1973)[29] has argued that, even when teachers protest vigorously that they treat all children alike, their middle class bias ensures that, albeit subconsciously, they treat middle class children so as to make for their success and working class children so as to make for their under-achievement. These performances by different children are directly the result of differential patterns of treatment during the socialisation process in school.

Such conclusions echo the findings of the schools studies of Hargreaves (1968) and Lacey (1970)[30] who found that once divided and labelled by the teacher, children respond to those labels by behaving in the expected fashion. This creates a self-fulfilling prophecy in teacher assessment of children and leads to a strong misconception about middle class and working class types which reinforces the belief that they should be treated differently.

Keddie (1971)[31] has given examples of how the teacher, whilst paying lip service to equality of opportunity, or even of compensatory education, does not in practice honour these asserted beliefs so, for example, whilst intellectually teachers accept that social class and ability are separate concepts, they do in practice causally relate them, assuming the higher quality of the middle class child.

A more telling, though more complicated example of this, shows how different patterns of socialisation are regarded by teachers as appropriate. Keddie goes on to claim that the most able pupils are defined by teachers as those most equipped to accept the teacher's own definitions of the situation. They are therefore pliant and accepting and easy to teach. On the other hand, lower achievers are inclined to question the teacher's assumptions, subject matter and presentation, trying to evaluate it in terms of their own socialisation and consequently disrupting the classroom. By causing problems low achievers are easily defined as unable to grasp the subject matter. By making life easy for teachers, the middle class child is taught to succeed, by making the teacher's job difficult the working class child learns not to achieve even though, according to the educationalist, the questioning, challenging child is really fulfilling a major goal of education.

In examining the procedures in schools themselves, the interpretive paradigm shows how the working classes are structured to fail without specific reference to or knowledge of family background or of any possible cultural deficiency.

Keddie (1971)[32] and Hopper (1975)[33] have argued that education need not be like this if less emphasis was placed on selecting and socialising children for an occupational hierarchy, and more attention was paid to the quality of different experiences, commonsense and background of the children, making for a much more flexible educational provision.

This still leaves us with the explicit Marxist claim that providing a lower quality socialising experience for some children is a deliberate plan to keep the lower classes in positions of powerlessness. Young (1971)[34] has argued that control exists in the exercise of the curriculum and in the ability of teachers to select out children on a basis of purely subjective criteria, and by the exercising of such manoeuvres as streaming or setting.

The curriculum, not regarded as an unassailable collection of immutable knowledge but as a social construct, is created to serve special needs. Thus the most complex, abstract conceptualisations become the curriculum for the high stream pupils, and the mastery of such conceptual skills is the criterion of

77

success. These become the conceptualisations accepted as quality in society and legitimised by the power structure. In the curriculum available to the lower streams, these areas remain untouched, and so there is no question of the lower stream child being socialised into the values behaviour and knowledge of success. Such knowledge is just not made available to them.

Education selects a few according to non-educational criteria and socialises them into the ways of the ruling groups. Access to such socialising procedures would be restricted of course, and restricted in school to those who come from groups which are identified as supporting the *status quo*. On these lines, Young argues that education is a powerful instrument of socialisation and social control. The teachers become a tool of the ruling class, representing a way of life and a form of socialisation which ensures the maintained disadvantage of undesirable groups.

These conclusions can be drawn from the interpretive model since through it nothing is taken for granted, and all aspects of the socialisation process are subject to scrutiny. This is an important feature of the approach since problems for study occur as work progresses, and simply because they are there, not because they are so defined by teachers or administrators. In fact it is an approach which asks some very awkward questions of our existing process of socialisation through education.

Nevertheless, the interpretive paradigm is open to a number of criticisms which counsel caution in accepting its analysis. These criticisms are aimed mainly at the theoretical concern of what constitutes valid educational knowledge, and the debate between immutable and socially constructed meanings. These need not concern us greatly here except in so far as the theoretical premises ultimately shape the analyses. It is sufficient to point out that the interpretive approach is not always clear, it is frequently self-contradictory and is unpragmatic in that it asks questions but suggests no answers.[35] Such criticism by no means renders the approach illegitimate but it does, rightly, indicate weaknesses of which the student should be aware.

The influence of social class: an alternative view of socialisation

The major contribution of the interpretive paradigm which has as yet gone unchallenged is the assumption that schools play a vital part in causing certain children to be under-socialised.[36] This, from the point of view of a discussion of school and socialisation, is important. What we are left with after consideration of the two lines of analysis, those of the normative paradigm concerned with social class and achievement, and the interpretive paradigm examining the school itself, is the inescapable conclusion that in combination these approaches show us that in our process of socialisation through education there are forces at play, which in ways that are still unclear to us create unanticipated latent consequences for many children.

Indeed, some writers argue that our traditional view of the school as an important agent in socialisation is misplaced. Jencks (1973)[37] doubts whether schools are capable of socialising children for either success or failure. Certainly there are plenty of examples of individuals who 'come good' in adult life after a poor school career. It is suggested that nothing can change the profound influence of family socialisation, and evidence from Jencks' comparative studies indicates that neither does family background influence ultimate success. His major factors turn out to be 'competence' and 'luck'. Schools, therefore, can be seen only as valuable in themselves, not as predicters of adult prospects of performance.

So we are finally offered the view that ultimate success in society is mediated through a variety of socialising experiences, and we have looked at some of these. Such experiences, received in varying measure by children in different circumstances are influenced by inequalities of social class, family life, by income, parental motivation and other environmental situations; they are influenced by the limitations of the school structure and teacher performance by sheer good fortune and basic competence.[38]

Adult socialisation

It is only fairly recently that serious study has been given to the socialisation process as it operates upon adults.

Traditional sociology tended to view socialisation as a function performed upon the individual during childhood, designed to ensure the harmonious continuity of society. The judgement of the end product of socialisation was, therefore, the performance of the individual as an adult in society.[1]

We have so far taken socialisation to mean the process of social learning which is more or less formally provided, and orientated towards future role performance. Not all learning comes into this category and, especially in a view of adult socialisation, much informal experience must be included as learning for social role play. If socialisation is defined to include only those learning experiences specifically designed for future social situations, then most of what is included in adult life would have to be left out of the account. If, however, the definition includes all the incidental situations which give us guidance in our lives, then even in traditional sociological terms socialisation in adult life becomes important. For the purposes of this chapter we will consider experiences in adult life which have some direct bearing on future values, attitudes and behaviour and these can be usefully limited into specific contexts which enable us more readily to connect up the learning with the outcome. Such contexts include political socialisation, job socialisation and the establishment of reliable expectations at home and in the community.

From the viewpoint of the symbolic interactionist there is no need for such debate. Adult socialisation is an inevitable aspect of the on-going life-long process of learning experiences through interaction with others. In this sense, fleeting as well as lasting relations assist an individual to develop skills and knowledge which he can build into the learning of future situations to enable him to fit more quickly and easily into the value and behaviour patterns of a new group. This can readily be seen for example in the reciprocal relationship between parent and child. When the first-born arrives, the learning which the child masters is staggering in its extent, but the parents too, particularly mother, are being socialised from this interaction to a considerable degree. That learning is used the next time a new baby arrives and though both baby and mother continue to socialise each other, mother's learning is neither so new nor so marked. She already has experiences on which to base new learnings. Before the first child her experience was probably no more than learning formal family, sub-cultural or school definitions of what mother's role should be, and this offers at best only basic guidance for the reality of the mêlée of family life with babies and young children.

In focusing more upon the adult in interaction, when considering socialisation beyond schooling the growing autonomy of the individual is apparent, how his developing self-awareness in relation to others with whom he comes into contact comes to set his own standards of social achievement. Largely according to these standards the adult adopts the behaviour of certain social roles which he desires to fill, and since many of those roles will conflict, as for example between father's role at home and his worker role away from home, much of his socialised experiences will be used to tread the tortuous paths between conflicting pulls upon him, many of which encourage new assessments and definitions of self.

This chapter will consider first of all these two main areas of socialisation pressures on the individual[2], first from the self, and secondly from others; then consider contextual socialisation influences on the adult, such as those of the political structure, the family, certain sub-cultural elements, the job and the organisation of work, the mass media and the local community.

From our discussion of the development of the self in the child[3] it was argued that Mead (1934) had clarified the importance of the individual's perception of his own self in the process of socialisation. Extending this essentially interactionist view into adulthood, we may see that some socialisation forces acting upon men and women are self-initiated; these may be in situations where one's self-image is not what one wishes and positive attempts are made to change it, or where a clear path of ambition is there to be trodden and which entails discrete role play and changes in values and behaviour.

In citing self-initiated learning as an important area for future study, Brim (1968) asserts that for some adults, changes in personality are more the outcome of the demands of the self than the result of the pressures of others.[5] Much self-inspired socialisation is in response to the demands of a society geared to achievement at work and the acquisiton of money and possessions. Some will therefore strive to learn the ways of economic success, others will work at the power game. Although such aspirations and learning are related to certain expectations of the wider society, they are self-directed in that the individual is ultimately the arbiter in assessing his performance. In many ways the self becomes a tougher task master with greater expectations than parents had ever been of that individual as a child.[6]

In interaction with others the individual is constantly experiencing new things, and if we see these experiences as being cumulative, each new situation requires further aspiration and further socialisation. In finding a way through these experiences the individual is autonomous both in deciding the way to go and in setting himself socialisation goals and procedures. Not only new people but new physical situations may require considerable re-socialisation or socialisation for the first time. Learning the invalid role is a striking example of a new set of circumstances necessitating a largely self-motivated new socialisation process. Dying[7] and growing old pose problems of adjustment too for the adult and new learned behaviour is essential in accommodating to society's expectations of the new statuses involved. It is little good saying like one of Arthur Miller's characters that one may be growing old but has no need to behave old[8]; others expect appropriate behaviour and, in the main, the demands of the self must harmonise with the wishes of others, for although we may differentiate between these two sorts of pressures they are inextricably interwoven. As our earlier discussions showed, the expectations of the self are founded in the expectations which significant others have of one's self. Whilst this may be manifestly true for the child, it may not be part of the meaning which the adult will attribute to his decision to pursue one course of action rather than another. The simple answer to this is that after such a complex socialisation behind him the adult has internalised the values of significant others and simply forgotten who those others were.

It is more straightforward to relate changes of status and role and the behaviour necessarily socialised therein to external influences upon the individual. These may be the responses to new situations related to an old role, such as learning the enhanced responses which colleagues expect of the academic with a brand new Ph.D., compared with the expectations of his former first-degree self. Newly married spouses may expect more from each other, compared with their cohabiting days. Alternatively, socialised behaviour may be a response to a new role situation such as a brand new maternal role or that of a newly promoted headmaster, both of whom have to cope with strange people and therefore fresh values, behaviour and expectations. The similarity is that whether dealing with the same people in new circumstances or new people altogether, the individual will, in interaction, be expecting and expected to learn new behaviour and attitudes.

In a society such as our own, the individual is from a variety of sources urged to respond to their pressure often for reasons which are not clearly specified. Many adults can identify quite a selection of sources which press for their submission. Those with the most powerful sanctions at their disposal, and therefore usually the strongest agents of adult socialisation, are the family and one's employer. Once having learned to respond in appropriate ways in these settings the adult is still faced with a battery of expectations from friends, neighbours, club members, drinking companions, political concerns, the mass media, the bank manager, the local church, colleagues at work, the one-time significant 'others' of one's childhood, subcultural milieux, advertisers, and so on. For many, the list will not end there.

Whereas the family in particular can make sustained efforts to ensure appropriate behaviour, the lure of the local pub may be sporadic, but easily more enticing, and the ultimate choices through the maze of pressure and counter-pressure are up to the adult concerned.

The adult undergoing socialisation is much less malleable than the child, especially the young child who responds almost automatically to the socialisation process and who, at a certain stage, is being virtually indoctrinated. The adult finds that most pressures on him are peripheral and the only skill he has to learn is how to balance out and accommodate to his satisfaction these various pressures.

Similarly, it is less appropriate in the case of adults to argue the efficiency of one particular socialisation pressure. Apart from the problems of separating and qualifying these forces, the goals are not so clear-cut as for example they are in the case of education for occupational status. Certainly there are agents of socialisation acting on the adult, albeit peripherally, which nevertheless are carefully calculated to get the process right. Much advertising on television is planned to produce a desired effect, and the appeal of most of it lies in the method adopted.[9] Very often a product is sold as a result of its appeal to the self-image of the consumer, an image which is often social class related. This sort of trick may equate a small car with well-to-do friends and a country cottage, or demonstrate how sweetly a certain drink goes with the most erudite of sporting pursuits and that elusive togetherness and intimacy between handsome man and lovely woman. At a much more extreme level, drugs and torture may be used to secure the desired behaviour in a political prisoner. Allegations recently coming out of Greece and Northern Ireland suggest this practice still widely exists in our otherwise apparently civilised Western World.

The shift from secondary schooling into education for adults in further and higher education reflects something of the change of process which our society treats as appropriate during a transitional period. For many young adults who left school early, their return to further education in college produces a surprise. Although the subject matter may be the same as in school and the ultimate goal some sort of examination grade, the other incidental socialising pressures built into the school day are absent in college. In that it is concerned with the making of the whole man and with socialising an individual who is probably unwillingly in school, schooling persists in fitting the pupil for this future place in society. Having left school, the individual returning to education finds these pressures absent. To his teacher he is now an adult and the special focus is no longer upon the process of socialisation, rather on the content with which the individual adult learner may do what he chooses.

It seems reasonable, therefore, to look at this tertiary stage of socialisation as largely context bound and through the substantive demands made upon the individual in certain of these social contexts.

Political socialisation

There is no rigorous formal framework of socialisation in our society which persuades people to adopt a particular political belief. Neither is there a standard process which imbues one with an overall political philosophy, or a particular party code. Political socialisation is markedly absent in school, and it is in the family and especially in early adulthood, that the impact of political ideas, if only incidentally, plays a part in the learning process.[10] The outcome of this form of political socialisation is that, in the main, British, and indeed American people are not greatly concerned with political issues or in taking part in political activities.

It has been suggested that loyalty to a political party is first transmitted through the family to the child, making greater impact on the adolescent coming up to voting age, and establishing itself in adulthood from pressure in the family, at work and in the local community. Butler and Stokes (1969) show that about 75 per cent of first voters go with parents' political choice but that over a period of time this blurs as other pressures bear on the individual's political decisions.[11] There is believed to be a traditional link between party choice and social class in this country, with a substantial number of working class voters voting Labour. Many working class people must inevitably vote Conservative, however, since a total working class Labour vote would ensure a Labour Government every time from sheer weight of numbers. Influences of social class on voting behaviour are partly the result of childhood value absorption and partly the outcome of pressures on the adult to conform to family and community values.[12]

The pattern seems to be that socialisation for a political system and for voting behaviour necessarily takes place in adulthood or, at the earliest, in adolescence, since no direct advice is given sooner. For many young people any tendency to learn political values is rebutted as middle class schooling combats home values, especially among working classes. As a result no party preference may be adopted even in the unlikely event that reasonable information on which to base such a choice is transmitted.

Tapper's (1971) view is that the grip which the socialising

pressures of class, school and stream have in shaping a realistic assessment of occupational opportunities is not matched in the shaping of political aspirations. In the absence of this guidance the adult may be open to strong political influence and such agents as trade unions, colleagues at work, as well as family and community tend to take the lead in this regard. Even these agents on the whole do not put on organized political pressure, although this is probably less true of the trade unions and certain occupational groups and, although apathy is not directly socialised, it may be the outcome of this rather inefficient programme. An example of another form of under-socialisation in our society. During adolescence and early adulthood a certain idealism, especially in colleges and universities, persuades many people to take up political cudgels and to understand the implications both of party politics and of the political structure as a whole. Much student activity is orientated politically, though it is rarely pragmatic except as it affects students' own lives. Higher education is possibly the only opportunity for many people to indulge in political whims in a supportive situation, and so some form of direct political socialisation is there for the taking. However, this only applies to the small percentage going into higher education and indeed only a small percentage of those will become involved politically. Of that involvement much will be concerned with immediate personal or community situations and only by implication with wider political and ideological issues.[13] For those who miss this experience and traditional forms of political expression, the initiative in adulthood is often drawn towards political involvement in the community. At the local political level in this country, this may mean as much as involvement in decision making on the local council or as little as simply a desire to understand and influence the matters which affect one's daily life at home. Often such political learning is motivated by self-interest or pressure within the family, but often also from a desire to be seen as one who helps others. This sort of political socialisation clearly may stem from a variety of

87

agents, which underlines the difficulties of examining adult socialisation as a process, and draws our attention instead to the substance of the demands made on the adult.

Political socialisation has developed into an area for study in its own right and brief comment in relation to adult social learning does it scant justice. Much of the work in this field, transcends traditional subject boundaries, and in addition useful research is being carried out in different societies so that a picture is being built up both of comparative political socialisation and the outcome of these forms on social systems and how certain value systems influence the processes of socialisation in special ways.[14]

Family socialisation for adults

A major facet of the socialisation of adults occurs in the family setting. New values, attitudes and behaviour connected to the special relationships of family life have to be established at three major junctures in adult life. Demands for change occur first with marriage then with the arrival of children in the family, and later, as death occurs, one spouse may have to cope with children or a surviving grandparent moves in and adjustments are inevitable. None of these changes are once and for all events. Continual learning to adapt takes place as a marriage develops, as children grow older and manifest adolescent problems, and later go on to leave home as adults. In later life, learning to live alone in widowhood is one of the most significant phases of adult socialisation, necessitating a stage of rapid adjustment often at a time when the individual has become thoroughly settled and socially routinised. Similar crises of adjustment occur upon divorce or separation, especially when children are still in the home, so that single parents have to re-learn the roles involved in providing a stable social situation for children without other adult support.

The relationship between partners in a new marriage places a significant demand for socialisation on the adult. At all sorts of levels and virtually at every minute of every day marriage is a learning environment, spouses adapting their whole selves to the character of the other, during the more or less continual process of interaction. New learning patterns are likely to be most necessary where the socialisation careers of the two partners are markedly dissimilar. This would occur, for instance, where marriages are made across class boundaries, or where cultural backgrounds are otherwise clearly different. This might happen in our society where an individual from the Home Counties 'stockbroker belt' marries someone from an economically run-down small Lancashire cotton town. Since social background has considerable impact on socialisation processes such different presenting cultures brought into a marriage will probably continue to require new learning on the part of both partners throughout their life together. There may be a variety of differences at the outset when, for example, language patterns may differ, and whilst it may be easy to adapt to words and idioms which are strange it will be less easy to agree which aspects of life are available for verbal expression. The way in which common experiences are conceptualised differently may well lead to conflict. Patterns of social life may similarly differ to a marked degree. The family companionship and sociability of the middle class way of life may not be adopted where the working class spouse seeks the company of friends of the same sex in the community. The possibility of doing this will vary with the community where the couple live and the 'wrong' environmental circumstances for one partner may put considerable pressure on him or her. Such pressures will be exacerbated by the experiences of the family of origin not being repeated in the new family, so that the working class partner, used to relatively little shows of affection and an interpersonal relationship which has been characterised as an exchange of services,[15] would be under great strain when a continual display of mutual affection is expected. Such instances suggest that re-socialisation for married life may have to be a fairly rapid affair to avoid a breakdown in the marriage. Indeed the divorce rate for marriages made between people of different social class backgrounds is relatively high.[16]

Among the characteristics of family life style which differ between the social classes in this country is the role of authority. Working class women typically wield power in the family whereas the middle class male is more dominant, although today equality in decision making seems to be becoming the rule. Where patterns like these are entrenched, spouses from different class backgrounds will have further problems of socialisation.

Apart from these fairly commonplace situations, there is a whole range of adjustments which although required in most new marriages is particularly difficult in inter-class marriages. Conversely the problems of socialisation of adults in family life are probably less for partners coming from similar homes and families with similar values and standards, levels of education, wealth and so on.

There are few indications of the outcome of the socialisation process during marriage. In fact the only indication beyond the family setting is that separation and divorce suggest a failure of socialisation. Such evidence is not reliable, however, and many other factors which bring about marriage breakdown may remain hidden. Pressures from religion and family of origin for example, may virtually enforce a marriage to stay outwardly intact even where there has been complete breakdown between the partners.

Often at a time when the respective roles of marriage are still causing problems and anxieties, the new role of parent is thrust upon the young adult. For some wives it may come as a relief to take on a role for which they have been better socialised. There is a belief that being a mother comes naturally to many women whereas being a wife is a job which has to be learned the hard way, through experience, trial and error. It is less likely that the new father has had any of the formal socialisation for parenthood that the mother had received. Girls often have had advice from their own mothers about bringing up a child, at the latest during their own pregnancies, and even many secondary schools devote curriculum time to dealing with mothercraft and home-making, though the success of such instruction needs further evaluation.[17]

Inevitably the learning of the parent role will differ for men and for women, and will depend to a large extent upon the degree of preparedness for the role which stems from previous socialisation. Parents who come from large families, especially where they have had childhood experiences of looking after young siblings, and this happens most frequently in working class homes, will not find the transition to rearing children of their own terribly hard. Such informal socialisation will sensitize the new parent to the needs of the baby in a way which has still to be learned by the parent who has had little previous contact with children. There is much more to the impact of the first child than simply adopting behaviours learned in other situations, and deep feelings hitherto untapped may ultimately mean that the personality of a parent will outweigh any socialisation, or lack of it, which the parent may have undergone.

It is unlikely that any mother or father is fully prepared for the demands which the new infant makes; even if they have had experience of bringing up young children they are likely to view the prospect of a new baby with a stylised, romantic vision. There is little that is romantic about the addition of a new member to the family and the demands made upon parents may be challenging in the extreme. At the same time as the baby makes his demands, so too do those individuals and groups who believe that they have some stake in the baby's well-being and who feel they have been involved in the socialisation process which has prepared the new parents for this experience. The strongest claimants to this position are grandparents, but other family members, neighbours, friends, health visitors and local clinic staff are judging the performance of baby certainly, and probably of parents too. So even at the earliest stages when the child is making few demands on his own and making little headway in socialising his parents, others have it in hand for him and are looking after his interests. All these pressures are greatest for a first-born child and, in some sub-cultural groups, most marked for a male child. Parents are clearly on trial, but what is essentially being tested is not an adaptation such as to the presenting culture of an adult male, but a total commitment to a whole person, which entails the subjugation of a previously learned established way of life. The pressure for socialisation of the parent, and the socialisation process to this end, takes place more or less at one and the same moment. This continues for twenty-four hours a day for months on end. It is likely to be the most intensive learning experience of adult life.

From the earliest days of family life of the first child, the mother and father begin to learn the appropriate behaviour in response to what Danziger[18] suggests are the child's two most powerful masks – the cry and the smile. With careful use of these two responses, the child can train his parents to behave in ways which he desires. It is a common assertion that parents change when their children are born, and here is one reason why, their offspring are socialising them into new ways. The socialisation relationship between parents and child, and particularly between mother and child, develops as a reciprocal dependence. Demands made by mother on the child, and by child on mother, encourage this dependence upon one another so that behaviour becomes increasingly orientated towards the development of that relationship. Limits are set by both parties as to what constitutes an acceptable or desired behaviour and within these limits the relationship develops along lines of compromise between the opposed wishes of both child and mother. As the child grows up the demands change in nature and complexity from the satisfaction of basic needs for food and warmth, to growth of language skills and guidance during the crises of adolescence. The parent, developing more slowly, learns to react to these needs, yet requires in turn to feel the warmth of the child's love and his dependence upon her. As the child becomes adult needs change again and are less clearly articulated, and eventually it is the mother who needs to learn the new role of not being the child's support any longer.

If the mother has played her developing reciprocal role in the upbringing of her children to the fullest extent of her capacity, then after twenty-five or thirty years, the loss to her of the last child through marriage means a significant new point of departure in socialisation. A form of learning matched for the male in retirement, an occurrence which may well happen at the same time as the last child disengages from the family.

For mother, the main activity in her working life has been building a relationship with her children, a procedure of socialisation which she never entirely masters, for as the relationships develop and the children grow older with new needs, so mother has to learn to adapt. Now, suddenly, all that ends. At best it may mean that the grandparental role will replace the parental role, and this will be especially true where children or grandchildren live with or near the original parents. Always provided that grandparental advice or interference is welcomed. This may be structurally built in to some subcultural circumstances, and Willmott and Young (1957) and Rosser and Harris (1965), have noted the special mother–daughter contact based upon continued domestic service.[19] Where geographical proximity between mother and married daughter persists, maternal interference is not always welcomed and, in these circumstances, learning the role of lessened responsibility and playing second fiddle to the daughter is a real socialisation problem which some mothers never overcome.

Generally, such learning problems are to do with the continuing relationship between mother and daughter, sons are more likely to live nearer to mother-in-law,[20] in working class circumstances particularly. Relationships between parents and sons are more probably economic in nature. Indeed it has become the cultural commonplace that the married man has problems

93

with his mother-in-law, and a music hall tradition of mother-in-law jokes is based on this view of the husband, though never of the wife.

Deutscher (1962)[21] has argued that the popular mother-in-law myth serves to pre-socialise parents into a readiness to accept the impending role and to avoid the conflict which might otherwise arise. In broader terms, Deutscher implies that American middle class parents learn to adapt to new post-parental roles by socialising experiences analagous to the family situation after children have left home to get married. Some of these experiences apply in Britain and may serve the same purpose. So when the adolescent is at college or university, or at camp with the scouts or on holiday with the boy or girl friend, parents, and particularly mothers, experience socialisation forces which prepare them for an imminent change in family roles. This way parents can develop early recognition of the new independence of their offspring.

Although this is a time of re-socialisation for adults it is not necessarily a depressing time, in spite of the mother's disengagement from her children. Studies in America have suggested that many people discover again the character and qualities of their marriage partner, especially amongst the middle classes, and this means that after twenty-five or thirty years of child rearing, re-socialisation is into a virtually new marriage, with deeper understanding, shared experiences and less individual social activity than hitherto. Post-parental life could be the most pleasant time for relationships in the family setting.[22]

Adults and school

There are various aspects of formal education which impinge upon the adult, directly and indirectly socialising him by so doing. As parents of school-aged children, adults are confronted by a range of socialisation forces from the school. Their experiences of these sources is, invariably, in conjunction with the educational performance of their child. Certain values will be transmitted through the child from school to parents. The example set by the child may encourage them to adopt certain school values. So, where the children of ambitious working class parents adopt school values and behaviour patterns it is not uncommon for parents to be similarly socialised simply by observing the child. Children will put more direct pressure on parents by expecting them to conform to the behaviour of the parents of other pupils, or from expectations generated by the school's own expression of normative parental behaviour, such as helping with sports day or paying for the cost of the terminal outing.

Schools also socialise teachers. As education becomes more a matter for debate and private opinion, and less a question of prescribed standards, contents and evaluations, teachers depend for guidance upon feed-back from pupils and colleagues. In this way, the development of the teacher's job role is shaped by the socialising pressures operating on him from pupils and colleagues, and this is increased as fewer traditional indicators remain in school. This may be especially true for schools working an integrated curriculum code.[23]

Direct contact between school and parent which by-passes the child is less common, outside of the private sector. Letters from the headteacher or from teachers may go direct to parents but these are likely to be about specific matters which carry little socialising weight. In meetings between teachers and parents, such as prize givings or parent teacher association meetings, deliberate attempts might be made to influence the behaviour of adults through the medium of the headteacher's speech or the nature of the ensuing discussion. At such functions, where a change of behaviour is demanded it is commonplace to hear the appeal prefaced with an acknowledgement that this is 'preaching to the converted'. In other words, it is implied that parents who attend meetings have little need to be socialised into the ways and values of the school, and this may put great normative socialisation pressure upon them.

Socialisation

Some aspects of the Plowden Report recommendations were partly aimed at socialising parents and the subsequent Education Priority Area project in Liverpool contained elements of socialisation for both parents and teachers.[24] The school-based coffee mornings were not only designed to show the parent that school was a pleasant meeting place, that the aims of the school were in harmony with the nature of the local community, and that the values embraced in school should be similarly espoused by parents, but also they made teachers aware of the problems of inner city life and enabled them to become closer to a real understanding of their pupils in school. This was an intention to socialise at two levels, an attempt which achieved only partial success as it perforce ignored many other environmental socialisation pressures which shaped the values of adults in the community of which the school was a part.[25]

In further education deliberate attempts are made to provide courses for adults aimed usually at achieving a qualification of some sort. Into these programmes little incidental socialisation is built. In respect of some forms of adult education Hopper and Osborn (1975) have noted that particularly women who miss out in education, do so partly because their goals and values lie elsewhere, and they return in adulthood to obtain educational standards suited to their abilities.[26] In some circumstances there is also a profound socialisation outcome. Many bright women, when their children are of school age take university and college qualifications and often grow away from their somewhat dull husbands or an already shaky marriage. Higher education serves to socialise such women into a new set of values which do not hold marriage and motherhood as the ultimate female achievements, and which will prepare them for competitive existence with men in occupational and social life.

Character training

It is difficult to decide exactly when the child becomes adoles-

cent and when the adolescent becomes adult. In most discussions the problematic of his assessment is not considered and
adolescents have been considered in some ways as children and
in other ways as adults. If we confine ourselves to a definition of
adults as those people beyond school-leaving age and not in full
time education, there is one other major form of education
deliberately designed to socialise young adults. This is the so-
called third arm of education which comprises character training
of the Outward Bound type.[27] Pursuits of this sort are linked in
that most of them provide facilities suitable for activities included in the Duke of Edinburgh Award Scheme. The aim of such
socialisation is often expressed as providing for the less for-
tunate, some taste of public school type education. Courses are
invariably run by middle class men who believe that experience
of physical challenge will have some social spin off for trainees.
In order to obtain trainees it is necessary to persuade sponsors
that courses costing over one hundred pounds for four weeks are
well worthwhile. Thus it is common to see claims that adventure
training directly benefits industry and it is in this context that
socialisation through adventure training is often seen.
Nevertheless there is a deliberate intention on the part of most
trainers to embellish the characters of those who come into their
care, and to offset the dangers of smoking, drinking and sex, to
which they believe the youth of our society regularly and meekly
succumb.

Socialisation forces in the local community

Living in a community brings the adult into frequent contact
with others at home and in the street, in shops, public houses,
clubs, parks, church and school, at parties and coffee mornings
and many more situations where individuals interact. As we
have observed already, different social situations will require
different types of conforming behaviour and in modern western
complex societies such as our own, there will be many new com-

munity situations which an adult will encounter for the first time and which will therefore imply socialisation.

Long stay within any one community is likely to entail the minimum of new learning for the adult resident as time goes by. Only the establishment of fresh community situations such as the arrival of new neighbours or the start of a new club; or more significantly, deeper changes in the character of the community such as the establishment of a new town on a rural village community, will involve pressure of re-socialisation upon adults to change their style of life.

Moving house to live in a new community may require conformity to different standards, such as styles of dress, speech, patters of sociability or community involvement. Socialisation of the adult in these circumstances will be in accordance with the values of others in the established community. Where the whole community is new, such as when a phase in a building programme is suddenly occupied, a pattern of interaction is set up over a period of time, as everyone adjusts to one another and early enthusiastic relationships break down and other more lasting friendship networks emerge. One of the problems encountered in re-housing city dwellers in new towns, even where there are attempts to keep old neighbours together, stems from the new environmental setting necessitating the socialisation of adults and children into fresh patterns of living. Socialisation which may inevitably involve the rejection of some old values, and some erstwhile neighbours. The evidence offered by the Bethnal Green study[28] suggests that strong pressures of socialisation were brought to bear on young families setting up homes in the housing development at Greenleigh to conform to the new estate life, and in many cases this involved a re-learning which threw aside the old values and attitudes of traditional working class East London.

Re-socialisation is likely to be least extreme for inter-community moves of a lateral sort, but moving house to another area which suggests upward social mobility may involve the aspiring adults in a range of learning appropriate to the new social class and community. Many moves, especially among young middle class adults, are from one home to a more desirable residence or a more prestigious community, and in such situations too socialisation is learning to respond to the expectations of others in the way which the community as a whole sees as legitimate and conforming. Geographical mobility may involve greater changes. There are many families in Britain who move from North to South and who are unable to fit into life in Southern England. Often such families quickly return North but even among those who remain many years living in a Southern community, there are some who are unable to adapt to the values and attitudes of those around. Inter-regional mobility can put a great degree of pressure upon the adult: pressure which may be greater than that involved in simple inter-class moves where aspirations include a mild anticipatory socialisation for the new situation. Inter-regional moves probably include no such aspiration. If, for example, the move is forced by the nature of the husband's work, wives may indeed resent the upheaval, be unhappy at being separated from friends and family and, in some cases still may be socialised into a distrust or distaste of people in the South or the Southern way of life. Feelings of this sort may make re-socialisation very difficult indeed.

At its most extreme, immigration into a new culture implies both immediate and long-term socialisation for adults. Most immigrants into this country from other lands bring with them a well entrenched presenting culture and in some cases a culture which has inbuilt resistance to ideas and values which do not conform. Adjustment to a new culture is a huge undertaking and in respect of American immigration Brim (1968) argues that the continuing American socialisation process for cultural adjustment is the greatest in history.[29] There are some useful reviews of immigration into Britain and many of these consider the problems of adjustment to a new cultural code.[30]

The range and depth of new cultural learning for immigrants is considerable, and although some needs are catered for in formal education,[31] other crucial re-socialisation occurs when the immigrant is left to his own devices and when the not always gentle pressures from the local community operate. The magnitude of this socialisation is such that some sub-cultural groups shun the new dominant culture, and live out their lives as far as is possible in communities based almost entirely upon the cultural patterns of their original homelands. This sort of life enables the immigrant to control to a degree the socialisation process to which he is subject by limiting it to that involved in essential contacts with the outside society. Some groups, for example Asian women, are able by their traditional position to cut themselves off entirely from contact with the dominant culture. Efforts to exclude socialisation pressures from outside may succeed in preserving dominant cultural values, but the education of the children of immigrants, who must attend the local schools, should, after one or two generations, mean that socialisation into the dominant culture is complete.

Some indigenous sub-cultural forces of socialisation directly encourage the individual into areas of behaviour which society rejects as deviant or even criminal. Although all individuals experience socialisation which implies adherence to an approved moral order, there may be a process working perhaps in family or community which teaches values and behaviour directly opposed to that moral order, or which rationalises that morality to socially unapproved ends. Where group values oppose societal values it is quite possible that the individual learner will be socialised into delinquent or criminal behaviour. Thus criminal behaviour may be socialised, approved and controlled by sub-cultural moral imperatives equally as powerfully as other groups enforce socially approved behaviour. Such pressure whilst negatively sanctioned by society can be seen as legitimate in that no one individual can ever know more than a small part of society, or of the process of socialisation which impinges upon him. So the person who manifests socially deviant behaviour is not necessarily under-socialised, nor unsocialised, though he may be either of these. It is quite likely that he is fully and efficiently socialised into deviant social norms through experiencing deviant values and behaviour. It can be argued that embracing the values of the sub-culture to the exclusion of those of the wider society suggests that the individual is, in some way, not fully socialised or fails to come up to the expectations required of full membership of society. Even to accept the powerful influences of family and community, the adult's values are the product of a cumulative process of socialisation in which it would be surprising if he did not encounter at some stage socialisation experiences which are basically anti-societal.

From an interactionist viewpoint the experience of deviant values are, in themselves, not automatically indicators of deviant behaviour and many such values are open to negotiation in the interactional market place. After all few children totally accede to the views of their parents, and few students support all the dominant values of society, but this is no prescription for patricide on the one hand or revolution on the other. Ultimately the individual, in the light of all circumstances, decides his own degree of variation from the normative style. The interactionist might argue that it is not until the apparently socialised individual sees himself labelled as 'deviant' or 'criminal' that he actually ends negotiation and starts to behave in a deviant or criminal fashion.[32]

Pressures such as these which transcend the line between child and adult socialisation and the community, and which lever the person into undertaking anti-social acts may succeed, especially where they are accompanied by labelling from 'approved' sources. Resultant diminished self-esteem can make otherwise responsible adults adopt attitudes and behaviour of a criminal or anti-social kind.

The effects of mass media

In considering elements of socialisation which impinge upon the adult, it is inevitable that much of what is discussed will equally apply to the socialisation of children. The effect of mass media is just such an instance where both adults and children are subject to a common impact. Radio and television, the cinema, newspapers and magazines are all powerful agents of socialisation. Watching television has become a central leisure activity. Even where it has existed for many years as in the United States and in Britain, and in competition with other attractive pursuits, it remains a major source of leisure time gratification. McQuail (1969)[33] has pointed out that there is a direct relationship between the spread of the mass media and a high level of societal development. In a democracy such as our own, television is widespread and simultaneously communicates the same message to a nationwide but well educated audience. Mass communication can threaten the rigid authority of a tightly controlled social organisation especially where a comparatively high proportion of the population hears the mass media message.[34] Whether or not close censorship is exercised, television is at least capable of socialising the masses by transmission of information and values.

The effects of the mass media depend considerably on shared meanings between broadcaster and audience. Once this channel is opened, it enables mass communication to by-pass social and interpersonal socialisation patterns and contact the individual directly. So neither the parent nor the school can prevent the child being socialised by television, any more than adults can avoid being socialised by the opinions of their favourite magazine or newspaper. The process of mass communication is so powerful that it has to be subject to laws and controls and be used where possible as a value-leader, as a conservative force for consensus in any effort of social control.[35]

Another view of mass media socialisation which is expressed

by sociologists is that it contains harmful experiences, particularly for children, but also for families in general. Too much television viewing is especially regarded as dangerous for children, and evidence is offered by Danziger that extensive exposure to pictoral fantasy is a base for therapeutic intervention.[36]

On the other hand, Himmelweit (1958)[37] and her associates played down the harmful and distracting effects of television on the child, and Larsen (1968) has collected a variety of discussions of the possible relationships between mass-media and forms of violent behaviour in an American context.[38]

The conclusions from much of the evidence gathered by sociologists are depressing. Apart from a superficial likelihood that general societal values will be transmitted, the socialising effects of mass communication, at least of the pictorial media, are latent consequences of devisiveness in the family, social isolation and self-delusion. In addition, it is often argued that this may be dangerously combined with the hypothesised tendency for television and the cinema to incite young people to crime and violence. This view is often put forward by magistrates and judges passing sentence on young people,[39] and tends to associate mass media socialisation with social unrest and decay.

Within this relatively small area of the influence of mass media upon adults, there are different theoretical viewpoints from which analysis may stem. Researchers working from psychological perspectives, have been interested in considering the effects of television and particularly television advertising upon children and adults, and suggest a number of possible cognitive effects of television. Many of these discussions are speculative since the problem of demonstrating any causal relationship is immense. Symbolic interactionists might focus upon the typifications of interpersonal relationships offered by the visual media. It would be surprising indeed if adults and children did not learn forms of behaviour by imitating television models. Such learning does, after all, take place by imitation from real life, and though no evidence exists causally to link interpersonal behaviour with television viewing or cinema going, neither could it be reasonably argued that powerful visual images from the screen cannot serve a similar purpose.

The role of advertising on television and in the cinema, as well as in print, is harnessed to socialising people into certain behavioural patterns, in this case, patterns of consumption. Unlike much mass media communication, advertising depends upon feed-back to evaluate the impact of an advertisement, and this offers the only real evidence of the effectiveness of mass communication as a whole. This has in turn stimulated a particular form of research in social science which considers the extent of mass media potential for socialisation and uses its findings to suggest ways of controlling that influence either to further the advertiser's own ends or to ensure that mass communication is carried out in the best interests of society at large.[40]

For any modern industrial society, as Galbraith (1967)[41] has pointed out, a major consideration is that both production and consumption must be planned. Herein lies the economic consideration underpinning the advertiser's activities; extend this a little beyond strictly economic pressures and we have a Marxist position which allots to mass communication a key role in manipulating imagined needs. Marcuse (1964)[42] argues that such 'false needs' are promoted to ensure inevitable acceptance of the existing social formation, and that only the removal of indocrination through advertising and of restricted transmission of information will free people to choose realistically the sort of society which they desire. Specifically in terms of advertising for consumption, he claims that the affluence of our present society depends upon production and consumption of waste and gadgets which all have limited life designed into them. The individual has to be socialised to adapt to integral obsolescence in the interests of uninterrupted production and preservation of the affluence of capitalist based society.[43]

Most of what can be said about the socialising effect of mass media upon adults stems from a traditional functionalist view, and most of what has been considered so far in relation to adults and socialisation media has been expressed in terms of function. Underlying this analysis is the assumption that society needs to receive and transmit information and to control norms and values in order to operate smoothly. This draws our attention to overall social functions, which although expressed through the activities of the socialised individuals, stress the needs of the society rather than those of the individual. McQuail (1969) argues that the interpretive approach to understanding mass media supports and elucidates the views of functionalist analysis. In citing Peterson's (1965) differentiation between objective and normative theory, McQuail concludes that objective theory sees the mass media in social interaction between individuals, exchanging symbolic values and beliefs, as between persons, and purveying in interaction both the stability of the society and the capacity to bring changes.[44] The interpretation of this aim in terms of achieved socialised goals is difficult to comprehend since 'preservation' and 'changes' seem to be concepts opposed. They are, nevertheless, the intentions not only of the mass media but also of education and are typical of the sort of aims verbally expressed by teachers and teacher trainers.

Interpreting the outcome for society, however difficult it may be, is more straightforward than understanding the outcome for the individual, although traditionally the recipient of mass media is seen as normal only within ill-expressed limits. Too much exposure to mass media and he is regarded as an escapist, whilst the non-viewer or non-reader is equally odd. This pattern implies that socialisation is self-justifying is so far as it builds in an element of what is considered to be justified. Exposure to the socialising agent is thereby limited within normative bounds. By the time we become adults we have had socialised into us the legitimate boundaries of exposure to that socialisation. This is more clearly illustrated in the case of mass media where the process comes up for scrutiny than where the goals are plain to the recipient, as in the case of education in school. Nevertheless, the relationship between the mass media and society is far from being clear and consequently its effect as an agent of socialisation upon adults and child remains problematic, and requires much greater study by sociologists.

Socialisation and work

There is a close connection between socialisation through the mass media and the individual's work situation. Many writers have noted that changes in patterns of work and employment have brought extensive opportunity for leisure pursuits.[45] Much of that leisure time is used in consuming mass communication, particularly television, and the growing relationship between socialisation through the mass media and life at work needs to be explored. Television may in itself provide a leisure pursuit but, with its power to socialise it may encourage both other uses of leisure time and a socially desirable attitude towards work which may or may not stimulate the worker to adapt to the processes of socialisation evident in his job.[46] It may not, for example, be thought socially desirable by media planners to encourage the membership of a trade union and adherence to the values therein, yet acceptance of the capitalist State may be always explicitly recommended. Whatever the inclinations of the mass media programmers, the socialisation of adults at work proceeds.

As in other new social situations, entry into a new job entails socialisation for interpersonal relations. These will be pressures similar to those experienced at school or in the community, except that certain specific interactions will have to be learned in order to regulate contacts between colleagues, or between workers and supervisor. Some of the learning will be specifically job related and consist entirely of factual information transmission, other learning may include informal organisation procedures, such as who has to sit with whom during meal breaks, or the rate of work accepted by the group.

Socialisation for working life may take place partly at school or, more probably, on the job. Many young adults change jobs two or three times during their first five years at work, and in so doing adjust themselves to the tempo of working life and ultimately seek out the job that suits them best. In many ways the adult uses this experience to socialise himself so that he may know better the grounds on which to base a realistic occupational choice. He has learned what suits him and what is available, as well as what constitutes the tenor or the work situation. Going to work for the first time, or changing jobs, entails both interpersonal socialisation and the learning of new occupational skills. In societies where work may entail becoming part of a large organisation, job socialisation can mean keeping abreast of the nature and demands of that organisation.

To pursue a Weberian model of bureaucratic organisation the variability and personality of the individual is virtually excluded.[47] There would be two forms of organisational socialisation for the individual once his technical competence placed him on a particular rung in the bureaucratic ladder, pressures to conform to the organisation and pressures for advancement in the organisation according to the further acquisition of technical competence. So however limited is the room for the vagaries of personality in this model of bureaucratic man, organisational work-life nevertheless has implications for personality. Although possibly individuals can ultimately change organisations through the stresses caused by the pull of the so-called informal organisation, it is more likely that organisations will either attract congenially minded workers or socialise workers to suit the needs of the organisation. Learning the occupational role in an organisation is going to be the result of a number of socialisation processes. The organisation will, in the Newcombs' (1950) terms, shape all the values and attitudes of the individual according to the position he is to occupy, and his behaviour will approximate to the specific requirements of the job in the organisation.[48]

Organisations are likely to include a series of demands which constitute a process of occupational role socialisation aimed at achieving the required behaviour from an individual worker and moreover the desire to behave in the appropriate way. The norms that are transmitted to that end are broad or specific depending upon the nature of the organisation, but the individual first learns the extent to which normative behaviour includes his own personal choices. In many cases the more restricted the choice and the greater the coherence between organisation and prescription, the more straightforward is the socialising message. Indeed it has been argued of teachers, for example, that they are more content in more highly structured circumstances.[49] As Levinson (1973)[50] points out, such normative organisational pressures are likely to include production rates, rules about employer and employee contact or worker and supervisor contact, even toilet arrangements may be rule-bound especially where temporary replacements have to be found for even the briefest absence. Levinson also offers a discussion of the socialising pressures placed on the individual by the conditions of work, and of the problems and dilemmas of interpreting the appropriate role which some jobs entail. These are some of a myriad of influences which constitute a complex impact upon the adult worker to encourage him to lead his everyday life in a particular style. As the socialising influences change, new learning takes place and the worker finds himself continually adapting to accommodate the requirements of the dynamic relationship between individual and organisation.

Social control

Just as the mass media implies manipulation of the populace and supervision of work entails restricting the spontaneous behaviour of individuals to fit the structural necessities,[51] so the whole of society uses the many processes of socialisation to ensure social harmony and continuity. In managing more extreme forces of individual behaviour and attitudes, socialisation can be interpreted as akin to social control. Although they are closely related, they are far from being identical concepts. Socialisation transmits, through the gentle and on-going manipulation of sanctions, a pattern of normative values, attitudes and behaviour which are essential for the preservation of social order. Social control depends largely upon the effectiveness of such socialisation for it operates when socialisation efforts fail and the individual or group indulges in acts which violate the dictates of the social or moral order. The general patterns of belief and action which are established by the socialisation process, especially during childhood, are developed by the growing individual to suit his own self-image. Socialisation has never been indoctrinatory except at the very earliest stages where the infant has no choice but to respond in certain 'social' ways. Even then, in adulthood, it is sometimes argued that individuals may reflect upon the processes which affected them as children and alter their attitudes and behaviour as they see fit. Such self-control is a form of social control with the socialised individual himself being the control agent. In appeal to this self-control, external agents may, for example, comment upon the irresponsibility of an action or behaviour as not being what might be expected from that individual, in the hope that self-control will prevent more dramatic uses of external sanctions. The close connection between socialisation and social control is emphasised by these examples.

In a society such as our own, adults will have experienced a great range of socialising influences and will manifest a wide range of values, attitudes and beliefs. Although all of these may be acceptable in themselves and tolerated by society at large, at the point at which they are in direct confrontation with opposing values forces of social control must be invoked to maintain peace. Since we do, in fact, tolerate a broad interpretation of what is socially normative, social control is an essential adjunct to our process of socialisation, which whilst universal, nevertheless operates in distinctive ways on different people, to produce varying and often conflicting results.

We are socialised, therefore, not only to our particular dispositions but into two forms of social control, one of which is self-control, the other being the recognition that society through social control agents should arbitrate in dispute. The variety of control agents depends upon the dispositions of individuals to accept the arbitration function of social control. There are situations rife today where society's agents are challenged by people who otherwise stress their regular acceptance of societal prescriptions.[52] When that socialisation is inadequate social control may involve an extreme repression of the views of the individual possibly by imprisonment or suspended sentence to serve as warning against further transgression. Socialisation may be more likely to be inadequate when it is society which requires particular behavioural response which may not always match the individual's own view of moral correctness. In that sense social control is much more a societal tool whereas socialisation is, as its name implies, concerned with making the social man. So in the work situation or at school, rules which govern the forms of communication between workman and supervisor, or between child and teacher in school, are more realistically expressions of social control rather than of socialisation. The difference between the work example and that of the school is that the teacher and child are interacting in a context where transmission of social and moral principle is the rationale behind the rule, even though both situations are organisationally, or at best societally, regulated.

In many respects it is possible to see social control as replacing for adults the socialisation process of childhood, one which permits the adult to see his behaviour in relation to societal need as, albeit temporarily, appropriate.[53]

Conclusion 6

Adolescence and social order

In the first part of this chapter some features of socialisation will be summarised in terms of their impact on the adolescent in society. The adolescent or youth phase of life lasts approximately from the onset of puberty to the formal acquisition of full citizenship which occurs usually at the age of twenty-one, although in Great Britain eighteen years is the case. In Western industrialised societies the phenomenon of adolescence is regarded as an important stage of socialisation which lasts for a period of some years. It is often believed to be an occasion when both males and females are at the greatest social risk; a period of transition when the individual is most liable to be beset by pitfalls and problems. Adolescence is popularly thought of as a time of deviance and unrest, when young people are likely to embrace anti-establishment values and involve themselves in violence and social confusion. Adolescence is a special time in functionalist terms because it occurs when much of the socialisation which has taken place in childhood has become internalised, yet when the adolescent is still searching for identity as an adult citizen in his own right. By the onset of puberty the individual has learned much about the nature of his culture, and particularly that section of it which belongs with his childhood roles and statuses, and from that cultural perspective he is searching for the adult roles and statuses to which he is heir. He has internalised the values, beliefs and attitudes of childhood, and once absorbed they are employed uncritically. At the same time he is exploring and evaluating values which as yet have no appeal.

As a child the world seemed unalterable and during childhood socialisation values were internalised in order that the individual could make use of his environment. Language is an example of a force of socialisation which is uncritically absorbed by the learner. This sort of internalisation, which Giner (1972)[1] has called 'instrumental', implies the acquisition of cultural forms without necessarily understanding or believing them. The second kind of internalisation, the 'critical' form, is one which enables evaluation to take place during adolescence. This latter kind of internalisation is typical of complex industrial societies where roles and norms may conflict to produce disbelief and give rise to actions based on the assertion that cultural norms are merely conventions and not in any sense immutable. This interpretation of socialisation is similar to Peters' (1964)[2] view of education as being first indoctrinatory and latterly a period of initiation which enables the individual learner critically to appraise what has gone before. Indeed during the school phase of socialisation some young people encounter subjects and structures which are geared to the development of critical awareness. This is often especially true in the fields of natural and social science. Although this critical perspective appears open-ended it is necessarily based on an assertion which underwrites the high status which we place upon scepticism in knowledge. However, not all adolescents will have been afforded the luxury in school of education for social evaluation. Many of them will first encounter this by contact with the mass media or through the anti-social stance taken by many peer groups.

Few adults question the functional model of socialisation which they have themselves been socialised to accept. Functionalists argue that predictability in socialisation is necessary in order to preserve the basic premises for human interaction. This argument is reinforced by examples which show that for any individual each new situation is freshly interpreted and defined so that in a small yet cumulative way a normative social change occurs. The idea that society changes is not always made clear to adolescents. Society still expects its young people to develop along traditionally established lines and, for example, stay in education until sixteen, long after physically maturity has been reached. This can mean not only a long period of economic dependence on parents with an attendant obligation to submit to their values, but as the onset of puberty appears at an earlier age as years go by, this span of adolescent dependence becomes longer. The notion that youth needs special treatment becomes stronger as the age of physical maturity lowers and the traditional socialisation resources of family and school becomes less effective. One response is to regard adolescence as no more than a temporary aberration, a time when normal relationships break down and when any eccentricity in behaviour has to be tolerated with gentleness and sympathetic understanding. A more positive view is that adolescence is a period when the individual is searching for an acceptable social identity which will ultimately enable him to develop a satisfactory adult self-image. This social identity will involve learning role performances the desirability of which the adolescent is unlikely to question. These have been the object of much earlier socialisation, and the boy's desire to be the breadwinner and provider for the family and to achieve the status which work and income brings is matched in the girl by the ambition to find a suitable life partner and settle into a pleasant family home with children.

In childhood the individual has been socialised to respect the expectations which others have of him. These expectations have helped to indicate the social roles which he will play, but the precise nature of these expectations will differ widely. During adolescence such ill-defined expectations may conflict with his own broad desires, and a self-image which varies depending upon whether he is with parents and family or with the peer group. For the first time in his life the young person is likely to regard the values of peers as more important than the values of parents, and the impact of the peer group is probably greatest during this youth phase of life.

Nevertheless, the influence of the family in socialisation is paramount, mainly because of its long-term nature and because of its privacy, and the process of socialisation started in the family is continued in education so that by the time the young person reaches his early teens in secondary school the more successful adolescents will have already been sorted out for future success. This preserves the existing *status quo* and controls the emergence of a new elite prepared for taking up powerful bureaucratic positions in society. The great majority of these successful young people will have been recruited from among the middle classes. The middle class is able to maintain its position of power in society largely through control of the education system. Inevitably it is only a few young people who are selected for future success and therefore many adolescents will find traditional education establishments inappropriate for their needs and values.[3] Emphasis upon intellectual achievement plus the inability of the school to cater for emotional growth has in the past been partly responsible for adolescent behaviour of an anti-social kind. When pressure to achieve or conform to certain standards becomes too great the adolescent may be forced to find personal satisfaction elsewhere and some may take up deviant activities. Many peer group relationships are available to support young people who fail to find meaning for their lives in family or school.[4]

The important role of the peer group in socialisation during adolescence is nowhere more dramatically illustrated than by the relationships formed by under-privileged groups of young people who for one reason or another find no stimulus or opportunity for self-actualisation in school. These peer groups develop largely as a reaction against their low status in life, exemplified by the few opportunities available to working class youth. Such rejection of accepted social standards is a limited attempt at revenge upon those who have ensured the second class citizenship of working class youth. In the past the cultural disadvantage of their social milieu has condemned them to a life on the dole or in a variety of dead-end jobs. In a society which rewards success following success with a fair degree of obvious affluence, those who are condemned to fail by circumstances beyond their control are by adolescence beginning to group together to hit at the whole fabric of achievement orientated society. During the economic difficulties experienced in Britain and much of the western world during the middle 1970s more drop-outs from middle class youth came to be influenced by the hitherto largely working class peer groups. These young people may express their views of society in violent ways, and by less overt expressions of aggression in their music and styles of dress. The leisure market available to adolescents reinforces the view that young people are qualitatively different from the rest of society. At one extreme, violence connected with music captured the headlines, and the emergence of punk rock as embodying the antithesis of traditional mass-marketed pop music whilst making a financially successful immediate future for groups like the Sex Pistols, has offered to the wider listening public concerts punctuated by foul and obscene language, and its young acolytes a distinctly adolescent art form. However, developments of this sort remain on the fringe of an adolescent leisure consumption pattern largely characterised by its economic importance. Most teenagers today have money to spend and manufacturers have paid serious attention to the buying power of young people to the extent of marketing clothes, drinks and entertainment designed especially to appeal to the young. The leisure orientated life style socialises adolescents into a pattern of consumption which is becoming widely accepted by society, and such a socialised adolescent is today very much the 'normal' adolescent. Socialisation promoted by a pleasure-seeking peer group is today largely accepted by parents as a natural stage in the growth of the young person towards adulthood.

In common with other socialisation experiences, peer group

learning is not passive, it requires the learner to participate fully in activities and subscribe to group values. Socialisation of this sort is facilitated when experience is consistent, and the peer group offers a consistent experience which transcends the efforts of family, school and the mass media. Easily available to the young person are styles of dress, music, literature, companions and adult models to satisfy his need for a normal adolescent experience. Although transition from school to work may be an inconsistency which makes socialisation traumatic at that point,[5] transition from childhood to adolescence is now made easy.[6]

This stage of socialisation for the adolescent is essentially a time when the individual is seen to be interacting with others, not simply as a passive recipient of information. Just as young parents are socialised by the new baby so the young adolescent has something to contribute to the peer groups to which he belongs. Negotiation of a role among peers enables the individual to develop a meaningful identity in that social setting and focuses attention again upon an interactive analysis of socialisation. Whether looking at socialisation as an interactive process or simply as a social function, it is usual to focus upon adolescence as a discrete phase in the growing-up process. Generally regarded as a period of rebellion and unconventional attitude which has been international in its extent, exemplified in the 1960s by the simple quiet parasitic life style of hippies and flower people which existed as a stark challenge to the gross economic ambitions of the western world, and in the 1970s by styles of dress functional for the rising tide of youth violence, adolescence exists as a challenge to society. This often effectively hides the fact that the majority of young people are conformist and well adjusted.[7] Particularly for those who come from middle class families their past prosperity and good future prospects encourage their social and emotional stability and a faith in the existing social system. Even among working class youth there are many who respond to society by working hard, getting as much as they can from educational opportunities, and taking their pleasure in the conspicuous consumption of leisure pursuits and electrical gadgets for the home. For these young people their link with working class rebellion is tenuous, and like their middle class conforming counterparts they are likely to regard the violent fringe as a threat to a society. Many of them are not politically active or even politically aware, they are unlikely to subscribe to the traditional working class views of the necessity for class struggle in society.

Concentration upon adolescence as a special period requiring a special process of socialisation has been contested by proponents of the adolescent myth thesis. This view points out that among educators, for example, there is little questioning of the view that young people possess distinctive adolescent attributes. In education there are special courses considered suitable for training of young people in desirable patterns of social behaviour. Such a course of action would never be considered appropriate for adults. For example studies of trainee teachers demonstrate shortcomings in that form of socialisation,[8] and study of character training demonstrates a similar failure on the part of trainers to be flexible in their thinking about adolescent needs.[9] The adolescent myth theorists suggest that labelling by society of adolescent traits does no more than promote the sorts of behaviour in young people which the labels imply. This view of the myth of adolescence might go some way to explain why young people do not seem to be greatly influenced in the long term by the special socialisation during adolescence.[10] It is possible that young people only play the adolescent game in order to fulfil the roles imputed to them but without ever subscribing to the values therein. This may explain why after the few short years of deviant social behaviour during adolescence the young adult settles down to a way of life closely identified with the outlook of his parents, the codes of his teachers and the beliefs of the wider society in general.[11]

Inequalities in socialisation

The inevitable differentiation in the socialisation process as it affects adolescents is the same factor which qualifies social learning for all other groups in our society: social class. Striking differences which have been discussed in connection with education operate at all levels in socialisation, and result in social class inequalities persisting or a division of labour, are reproduced generation after generation. In modern western societies where physical possession of capital plays only a small part in defining class differences the acquisition of educational excellence is paramount. Such credentials are not inherited, they are passed on at home and in school, in short, through the socialisation process.

Moving away from a functionalist interpretation of socialisation permits a view of socialisation as an important process in legitimising a class structure based on credentialising. Socialisation in our society is amenable to a Marxist interpretation, but until recently this has commanded scant attention in sociology. A Marxist interpretation points out that socialisation may restrict aspirations and opportunities as well as advancing them, whereas functionalism emphasises the stability of the social system rather than the need for any social change. Our analysis of socialisation so far has been from a broadly functionalist perspective, which conveives of the process as one discrete entity of an overall social system. It is relatively easy to understand social categories as having static definable boundaries and to ignore the outcome of change which takes place in society. The functionalist model of the social system assumes an interrelatedness of the parts of the whole. Socialisation therefore has been in terms of its special contribution to the operating of the whole social system. The way in which we have analysed socialisation as been to explore some of the workings of the process and their effects in relationship to society. It is only through a theoretical form which permits the understanding of components of the social system as being able to operate independently that the effectiveness of social action promoted through the process of socialisation can be assessed. Other forms of analysis which stress interrelatedness of the parts of society, such as an interactional perspective, emphasise the inappropriateness of looking at socialisation as a discrete entity.

A Marxist emphasis upon relations between various aspects of the social system would claim that any one social context includes within itself elements of the others. Therefore socialisation includes elements which are economic, political, moral and legal as fundamental and essential parts of the process of social learning.

Although for the student coming to sociology for the first time it makes good sense to take for granted the way in which analysts of society are able to compartmentalise the social system in order to understand it, it is nevertheless important at the end of such a process to ask what would be implied if we thought about society as being made up of interrelated elements. One of the main reasons for doing this is that it occurs even to the most naive student that abstraction of a single aspect of society, inevitably removing it from it social context, lends us a false focus of interpretation. Indeed as many researchers point out, the choice of any subject for study reflects their interest and belief that one piece of society is worthwhile for investigation. Studying the relationships which may exist between items in society usually treated as discrete may be argued to be an attempt at transcending the normal boundaries of theoretical background to investigation. Although any Marxist approach is itself ideologically restricted, some of its application nevertheless attempts to relate aspects of the social system across traditional boundaries.

Some examples of this separation taking place in studying socialisation include consideration of problems like language learning, authority relations in school, social class background in the home, the influence of the social services, or new learning at work, when these are all seen as independent topics. This presents to students an uncritical view that separatedness in society is an acceptable interpretive form. Indeed, more seriously, these separate forms of the elements of society, having once been studied, are then often used as evidence for the need for practical intervention, or administrative change. When such forms of social intervention fail it may well be because the original data failed to account for the relationship between that element of society and all others.

By so broadening the field of socialisation to include related elements in society we inevitably spread ourselves more thinly on the research ground. This means that relational studies are likely to emphasise particular influences in particular contexts. It is only after subscribing to the view that the relational style of investigation is essential that we can tolerate this sort of otherwise superficial analysis. Such broad study might focus, for example, upon the single aspect of selection through socialisation; the way in which the existing social order is maintained and existing hierarchies perpetuated.

Social selection through socialisation takes place within a framework of criteria based upon ill-defined community standards. As has already been pointed out standards of knowledge may well be related to the interests of certain power groups, and although it may appear that standards of knowledge are absolute, the model which claims their relatedness to a power structure which includes labour, private property and so on, enables us to see that a functionalist view of socialisation may ignore important related issues. So, for example, circumstances may permit some communities to socialise according to perfectly appropriate standards which other groups would nevertheless find intolerable. In such a case, the nature of socialisation can be justified in terms of values which lie much deeper than the simple process of socialisation itself. This implies that although social standards seem obvious and appropriate in any judgement of socialisation, they may indeed be deeply hidden in a firmly entrenched social, moral and political myth. In Marxist terms, that myth which enables evaluation to take place through socialisation is one based upon a positivist science and capitalism which enables labour to be alienated in a situation where every individual in society becomes objectified as a commodity. It can be argued that the nature of the boredom and meaninglessness of the lives of many people stems from a process of socialisation and other social evaluation which enforces the separation of one individual from another. The stress which we place upon achievement and ranking, privatises life to such an extent that each child stands separate from every other.

Individuality is inevitably built into the process of socialisation in our society. Children are encouraged to compare themselves with other individual children and the concept of individuality is one which the child soon understands in orientating himself to home, school or work. For all our efforts to develop new ways of teaching in school based on far-seeing ideals of socialisation the process is nevertheless only judged in terms of individual achievement or how well little children are able to do on reading or arithmetic tests. The problem involved in any sort of co-operative socialisation project is that in order to assess it it has to be torn apart to fit a framework of individualised evaluation.[12] If as sociologists we are to contribute anything further to our understanding of socialisation it may be to point out that there are inherent dangers in looking at the individual as the fundamental social unit. The reductionism tendencies in psychology are implicitly criticised in the approach of the sociologist to his subject matter. Yet even from the perspective of a Marxist orientated sociologist, it is clear that our process of socialisation stresses individual qualities.

In the family each child is treated by his parents as having essential worth as an individual rather than just a family member. Once the child has grown out of babyhood he is being groomed by his parents for a life of resourcefulness and achievement based upon standards mirrored in education, at work and elsewhere in society. With the gradual disappearance of extended family networks in our society parents are encouraging the individual achieving qualities of children so that attitudes may develop to enable each child successfully to make his own way in the world.

Parents, and increasingly teachers, are not pursuaded that the flexibility of group project work in schools is socially desirable; most of them recognise that the ultimate evaluation of schooling is based upon the number of C.S.E. or O level grades obtained.

Socialisation into an ideology of individualism proceeds not only in education but in many other aspects of society which the child observes. We hold individuals responsible for crimes and they are punished as individuals; the mentally ill are treated and released alone, and even where some group therapy does take place in hospitals, the ultimate decision about release is based upon assessment of the individual.

Children quickly learn to rank themselves in relation to others according to criteria which are presented to them. In education they are ranked according to the way they reproduce knowledge, they are not expected to produce it of theselves, rather they are socialised into a receptive condition. Children are encouraged to accept the world as it is as a given absolute. Dependence upon individualism as a process of assessment is facilitated by the notion that there are certain appropriate attitudes and behaviour suited to each individual's social situation, and so not only are the child's personal preferences influenced, but so too is his sense of the possibilities open to him in society. By this notion of individuality it is possible to preserve a form of social order where some people have much power, and others have none.

Marxists might argue that through evaluation the products of the child's work in school can be seen as a commodity. Since at various stages in the socialisation process the individual is subjected to evaluation, it is easy to understand social learning as a product to be ranged alongside other products, compared with the achievements of others. Children, therefore, see their efforts in terms of value as units of exchange. The achievement of the person loses its individual purposiveness and becomes worthwhile only in relation to what others achieve. Viewing socialisation from a Marxist standpoint it may be argued that the pupil's learning and achievement is seen as not his personal self-motivated production but as being dependent upon others who evaluate and select what is worthwhile. In this sense, socialisation is alienation. Only certain parts of our whole selves are regarded as worthy and these are therefore developed as a market place commodity. Thus creative potential in an individual is neglected.[13]

Without the awareness which this Marxist position implies it is commonplace for the pupil to be understood as a passive recipient of the socialisation process where socialisation itself becomes the transmission of items from a bank of social knowledge. This bank of social knowledge is introduced to the individual by someone who is expert, only because they have themselves drawn from that bank of knowledge for many years. Evaluation of both learner and teacher then becomes an important socialisation technique, which represents a return to the ideal functionalist position which sees parts of the social whole as separate entities. Partly as a result of this view it is argued that our complicated society, like all advanced industrial society, needs a form of bureaucratic grading, and that therefore examinations are unavoidable. The belief is that complex societies' like our own cannot function without a highly developed system of evaluation, and that such evaluation sets the seal on the process of socialisation which we all undergo.

If we think of the product of socialisation as being cultural capital possessed as a commodity by individuals it is easy to support Bernstein[14] who concludes that children are socialised at an early age into viewing knowledge as private property. In the same way the attributes fostered through socialisation become equally private, and not only is school knowledge regarded as being of such high status that it is worth hiding from one's neighbour, but so too is the knowledge transmitted by the society at large. Much of what we learn at home is designed to facilitate our selection for future high status. Most of what we learn at school is limited, and some pupils are evaluated in such a way, as Keddie[15] has pointed out, that knowledge which is selected for them gives them privileged access to success. At work we may have the need to possess the knowledge to control our own affairs only to find that this knowledge is denied to us and the best illustration of this division in society is the manifestation of class. If class differences were to disappear so too would the differences between high status and low status socialised knowledge, a difference well illustrated by the distinction between mental and manual knowledge. The reification of social relations which this distinction implies is thoroughly supported by the existing forms of socialisation in our society. By looking first at the position of young people, and secondly at the evaluative process as it works in socialisation we are left with an impression of injustice which is bred through the treatment of individualism as an ideology, of the objectification of personal production, of the conception of socialised knowledge as property and ultimately of alienation fostered by the process of socialisation.

Many Marxists would dissociate themselves from these views. They are necessarily brief and do scant justice to a highly developed social theory. Such a position does, however, serve to illustrate that the comfortable analysis of socialisation usually promoted and the one which has been maintained in most discussions in the foregoing chapters is indeed the analysis of the functionalist. What has been said many times before bears repeating; there are many different forms of socialisation, differing between family and family, class and class, society and society, different forms which are ultimately understood through analysis from one particular theoretical or ideological standpoint. Different standpoints will emphasise different aspects of this most variable of social processes.

References

Chapter 1   The meaning and uses of socialisation

1. Child, I. L. (1943) *Italian or American*, Yale University Press, pp. 18–19.
2. Ogburn, W. F. and Nimkoff, M. F. (1940) *Sociology*, Houghton Mifflin.
3. Elkin, F. (1960) *The Child and Society*, Random House, New York, p. 4.
4. Chinoy, E. (1961) *Society: An Introduction to Sociology*, Random House.
5. Wrong, D. (1961) 'The over-socialised conception of man in modern society', *American Sociological Review* **26**, 184–93.
6. Parsons, T. (1955) 'The American family: its relations to personality and the social structure', in Parsons, T. and Bales, R. F. (1956) *Family, Socialisation and Interaction Process*, Free Press, New York, p. 321.
7. See for example Parsons, T. (1950) 'Psychoanalysis and the social structure', in Parsons, T. (1954) *Essays in Sociological Theory* Collier – Macmillan.
8. Durkheim, E. (1953) *Sociology and Philosophy*, Free Press, New York.

9. Mead, G. H. (1934) *Mind, Self and Society*, University of Chicago Press.

10. Cook-Gumperz, J. (1973) *Social Control and Socialisation – A Study of Class Differences in the Language of Maternal Control*, Routledge and Kegan Paul.

11. Bernstein's work, and that of his colleagues at the University of London, Institute of Education, Sociological Research Unit appears in the series edited by Bernstein: Bernstein, B., *Primary Socialisation, Language and Education*, Routledge and Kegan Paul.

12. Cooley, C. H. (1902) 'The looking glass self' in Cooley, C. H., *Human Nature and the Social Order*, Scribners. New York. Also in Manis, J. and Meltzer, B. eds, (1967) *Symbolic Interaction*, Allyn and Bacon, Boston.

13. Mead, G. H. (1934) op. cit. [*ref. 9 above*].

14. Clausen, J. A. (1968) 'The history of socialization studies' in Clausen, J. A. ed, *Socialization and Society*, Little Brown New York.

15. This indebtedness to Mead is exemplified in Davis, K. (1948) *Human Society*, Macmillan, New York. Davis acknowledges in a footnote (p. 209) that a substantial section of his Chapter 8 is paraphrased from Mead's 'brilliant discussion'.

16. Danziger, K. (1971) *Socialisation*, Penguin Books.

17. Danziger, K., op. cit. p. 13.

18. Isaacs, S. (1933) *Social Development in Young Children*, Harcourt Brace, New York.

19. Kardiner, A. and Linton, R. (1939) *The Individual and his Society*, Columbia University Press, New York.

20. Murphy, G., Murphy, L. B. and Newcomb, T. M. (1937) *Ex-*

perimental Social Psychology, Harper, New York. Title to Part Two, 'The interpretation of the process of socialization'.

21. Writing particularly about the adolescent learning social roles, see Parsons, T. (1942) 'Age and sex in the social structure of the United States', *American Sociological Review,* **7**, 604–16.

22. Ogburn, W. F. and Nimkoff, M. F., op. cit. [*ref. 2 above*].

23. Ogburn, W. F. and Nimkoff, M. F. op. cit. [*ref. 2 above*].

23. Davis, K. (1948) op. cit., Part Two, and especially Chapter 8, 'Socialization' [*ref. 15 above*].

24. MacIver, R. M. and Page, C. H. (1949) *Society: An Introductory Analysis,* Macmillan. Although Chapter 3, 'The individual and society' covers substantially the same ground as Davis' (1948) [*see ref. 15 above*] work, and uses broadly the same references, no mention is made of the concept of socialisation. This may reflect the extent to which the term had not been universally accepted into sociology even in the late 1940s.

25. Davis, K. (1948) op. cit., p. 208 [*ref. 15 above*].

26. Cooley, C. H. (1902) op. cit. [*ref. 12 above*].

27. Grant, M. (1974) *Vanya,* Victory Press. This work is an account of the sufferings of one man under torture in Russia, for anti-Soviet beliefs.

28. Two examples of feral children appear in summary in Davis, K. (1948) op. cit., p. 204 ff. [*ref. 15 above*].

29. Mead, G. H. (1934) op. cit., p. 175 [*ref. 9 above*].

30. Fletcher, R. (1971) *The Making of Sociology,* Vol. 2, Nelson University Paperbacks.

31. Meltzer, B. N. (1967) 'Mead's social psychology' in Manis, J. and Meltzer, B. N. ed, op. cit.

32. Kardiner, A. (1945) *The Psychological Frontiers of Society,* Columbia University Press.

33. Seers, R., Maccoby, E. E. and Levin, H. (1957) *Patterns of Child Hearing,* Row Peterson. See also examples in Danziger, K. (1971) op. cit., pp. 24–6 [*ref. 16 above*] and in Danziger, K. ed., (1970) *Readings in Child Socialization,* Pergamon.

34. A useful discussion of this trend in American psychology appears in Danziger, K. (1971) op. cit., pp. 154–7.

Chapter 2 Child socialisation: the family setting

1. See for example: Douglas, J. W. B. (1964) *The Home and The School,* MacGibbon and Kee; Floud, J., Halsey, A. H. and Martin, F. M. (1956) *Social Class and Educational Opportunity,* Heinemann. Excellent summaries of these and similar studies appear in Banks, O. (1973) *The Sociology of Education,* Batsford.

2. Farmer, M. (1969) *The Family,* Longman.

3. Farmer, M., op. cit., p. 81.

4. A possible exception to this standard pattern may exist on Israeli Kibbutzim, where adult models other than parents assume the socialising role.

5. The tendency for delinquent boys to be rejected by their fathers is noted in: Andry, R. G. (1962) *Paternal and Maternal Roles and Delinquency,* W.H.O. Public Health Papers, 14, Geneva; and Andry, R. G. (1960) *Delinquency and Paternal Pathology,* Methuen, London.

6. Bromley, P. M. (1971) *Bromley's Family Law* (4th edn), Butterworths. There is a common law duty on the part of the

parent to provide physical care for the child up to the age of sixteen, and beyond that in cases of infirmity or other forms of dependence.

7. Trends in the style of child upbringing are discussed by a number of authors including Farmer, M. (1969) op. cit., and Shipman, M. D. (1972) *Childhood: A Sociological Perspective*, N.F.E.R. Publishing Company London, and Dreitzel, H. P. ed., (1973) *Childhood and Socialisation*, Collier-Macmillan.

8. Davis, K., op. cit. [*ref. 15, Ch. 1*].

9. B.B.C. 2 'Horizon' programme of 3 May 1976, 'Why did Stuart die?'

10. Farmer, M. (1969) op. cit., pp. 95–6 [*ref. 2 above*].

11. Hartup, W. W. and Zook, E. A. (1960) 'Sex role preferences in three and four year old children', *Journal of Consultative Psychology* **24,** 420–6.

12. See for example Michel, W. (1967) 'A social learning view of sex differences in behaviour', in Maccoby, E. *The Development of Sex Differences*, Tavistock.

13. Kohlberg. L. (1967) 'A cognitive developmental analysis of children's sex role concepts and attitudes', in Maccoby, E., op. cit.

14. Weitzman, L. (1972) 'Sex role socialization in picture books for pre-school children', *American Journal of Sociology* **77,** no. 6.

15. See for example: Adams, C. and Laurikeites, R. (1972) *The Gender Trap*, Book One, 'Education and Work,' Virago Paperbacks; Sharpe, S. (1976) *'Just Like a Girl: How Girls Learn to be Women,* Penguin Books; Rowbotham, S. (1971) *Woman's Consciousness, Man's World.* Penguin Books; Rowbotham, S. (1973) *Hidden from History*, Pluto Press.

Chapter 3   Child socialisation: school and beyond

1. Stenhouse, L. (1971) *Culture and Education*, Nelson University Paperbacks, p. 3.

2. See for example Nash, R. (1971) 'Camouflage in the classroom', *New Society* **18**, 447, 667–9.

3. Hopper, E. and Osborn, M. (1975) *Adult Students*, Routledge and Kegan Paul.

4. Nash, R. (1973) *Classrooms Observed*, Routledge and Kegan Paul. Also Keddie, N. 'Classroom knowledge', in Young, M. F. D. ed., (1971) *Knowledge and Control: New Directions for the Sociology of Education*, Collier–Macmillan.

5. Banks, O. (1955) *Parity and Prestige in English Secondary Education*, Routledge and Kegan Paul.

6. See for example, Douglas, J. W. B. (1964) op. cit. [*ref. 1, Ch. 2*].

7. Banks, O. (1973) op. cit., p. 32 [*ref. 1, Ch. 2*].

8. Levitas, M. (1974) *Marxist Perspectives in the Sociology of Education*, Routledge and Kegan Paul, p. 39.

9. See for example, Veness, T. (1962) *School Leavers: Their Aspirations and Expectations*, Methuen, London.

10. The range of knowledge which is made available may also be construed as a force of socialisation. See Chapter 4.

11. White, G. E. 'Aspects of transition from school to work', Unpublished M.A. thesis, University of Liverpool.

12. See for example, Hargreaves, D. (1968) *Social Relations in a Secondary School*, Routledge and Kegan Paul.

13. See for example, Coleman, J. (1961) *The Adolescent Society*, Free Press.

14. Gerth, H. H. and Mills, C. W. (1948) *From Max Weber: Essays in Sociology,* Routledge and Kegan Paul.

15. This, and other aspects of education provision in England and Wales are summarised in White, G. E. (1975) 'Education', in Mays, J. B., Keidan, O. and Forder, R. A. D. eds *Penelope Hall's Social Services of England and Wales* (9th edn) Routledge and Kegan Paul.

16. Some famous exceptions include Michael Duane's experiences at Risinghill School in London, documented in Berg, L. (1966) *Risinghill; Death of a Comprehensive,* Penguin Books. Also the recent events at the William Tyndale school and the efforts of the headmaster, Terry Ellis. Since the first inquiry into the latter example there have been calls for greater Central Government control in education, something which is traditionally at variance with the English system. See for example: *The Guardian,* 13.10.76; Ellis, T. McWhirter, J., McColgan, D., and Haddow, B. (1976) *William Tyndale, the Teachers' Story,* Writers and Readers Publishing Corporation.

17. Young, M. F. D. (1971) op. cit. [*ref. 4 above*].

18. See for example, Meade, M. and Calas, E. (1955) 'Child training ideals in a post-revolutionary context; Soviet Russia,' in Meade, M. and Wolfenstein, M. *Childhood in Contemporary Cultures,* University of Chicago Press, pp. 179–203. See also Grant, N. (1965) *Soviet Education,* Penguin Books.

19. Durkheim, E. (1963) *Education and Sociology,* Free Press.

20. See for example, Bordieu, P. (1971) 'Systems of education and systems of thought', in Young, M. F. D., op. cit. [*ref. 4 above*].

21. Lacey, C. (1970) *Hightown Grammar,* Manchester University Press; and Hargreaves, D. (1968) op. cit. [*ref. 12 above*].

22. Examples include, in this country the Education Priority Areas project, set up in the wake of the Plowden Report, and in America, Project Headstart, established during the administration of Lyndon Johnson.

23. Nash, R. (1973) op. cit. [*ref. 4 above*].

24. Halsey, A. H. (1972) *Educational Priority*, Vol. 1, H.M.S.O.; Halsey, A. H. 'E.P.A. go away . . . come again another day', priorities in urban education, *The Guardian* 4.12.73; Midwinter, E. (1972) *Priority Education: an Account of the Liverpool Project,* Penguin Books; Midwinter, E. (1973) *Patterns of Community Education,* Ward Lock; Midwinter, E. (1975) *Education and the Community,* Allen and Unwin.

25. See for example, Himmelweit, H. (1966) 'Social background, intelligence and school structure; an interaction analysis, in Meade, J. E. and Parkes, A. A. eds, *Genetic and Environmental Factors in Human Ability,* Oliver and Boyd. See also Turner, R. (1964) *The Social Context of Ambition,* Chandler, San Francisco.

26. Adorno, R. et al. (1969) *The Authoritarian Personality,* Norton, New York; and Lewin, K., Lippett, R. and White, R. K. (1967) 'Patterns of aggressive behaviour in experimentally created social "Climates",' in Amidon, E. and Hough, J. *Interaction Analysis,* Addison-Wesley, New York.

27. See Clausen's discussion of American research in this field in Clausen, J. A. ed., op. cit., p. 163 [*ref. 14, Ch. 1*].

28. Lacey, C., (1970) op. cit. [*ref. 21 above*].

29. See for example: Cohen, S. ed. (1971) *Images of Deviance,* Penguin Books; Taylor, L. (1971) *Deviance and Society,* Joseph, London.

30. Turner, R. (1961) 'Modes of social ascent through education', in Halsey, A. H., Floud, J. and Anderson, A. A.

eds, *Education, Economy and Society: A Reader in the Sociology of Education*, Free Press, New York.

31. Wilkinson, R. (1964) *The Prefects: British Leadership and the Public School Tradition*, Oxford University Press.

32. Bernstein, B. (1969) 'The classification and framing of educational systems', in Young, M. F. D. (1971) op. cit. [*ref. 4 above*].

33. Freire, P. (1972) *Pedagogy of the Oppressed*, Penguin Books.

34. Illich, I. (1970) *De-schooling Society*, Penguin Books.

35. See for example: Richmond, W. K. (1973) *The Free School*, Methuen, London; Bowles, S. and Gintis, H. (1976) *Schooling in Capitalist America*, Routledge and Kegan Paul; and Dore, R. (1976) *The Diploma Disease*, George Allen and Unwin.

36. Anderson, R. C. (1963) 'Learning in discussion: A resume of the authoritarian–democratic studies' in Charters, W. W. and Gage, N. L., *Readings in the Social Psychology of Education*, Allyn and Bacon, New York.

37. Gorbutt, D. (1972) 'The new sociology of education', *Education for Teaching*, Autumn, 1972.

Chapter 4   The influence of social class: an alternative view of socialisation

1. Burt, C. (1937) *The Backward Child*, University of London Press; Burt, C. (1975) *The Gifted Child*, Hodder and Stoughton.

2. Included among the studies into the influence of social class upon achievement in school are: Douglas, J. W. B. (1964) op. cit. [*ref. 1, Ch. 2*] and Central Advisory Council for Education (England) (1954) *Early Leaving*, H.M.S.O. A summary

of study data in this field appears in Westergaard, J. and Little, A., 'Educational opportunity and social selection in England and Wales: trend and policy implications' in Craft, M. ed. (1970) *Family, Class and Education, A Reader*, Longman. Also in Central Advisory Council for Education (England) (1960) *Fifteen to Eighteen*, The Crowther Report, H.M.S.O.

3. Douglas, J. W. B. (1964) op. cit. [*ref. 1, Ch. 2*].

4. Jackson, B. and Marsden, D. (1966) *Education and the Working Class*, Penguin Books; Floud, J., Halsey, A. H. and Martin, F. M. (1956) op. cit. [*ref. 1, Ch. 2*].

5. *General Household Survey* (1973) H.M.S.O., para. 233.

6. Schools' Council Working Paper No. 27 (1970) 'Cross'd with adversity: the education of socially disadvantaged children in secondary schools', Methuen, p. 127.

7. Flude, M. (1974) 'Sociological accounts of differential educational achievement', in Flude, M. and Ahier, J. *Educability, Schools and Ideology*, Croom Helm, London.

8. Bossio, V. (1971) 'Language development and reading attainment of deprived children', in Kellmer Pringle, M. *Deprivation and Education*, Longman.

9. Bernstein, B. (1969) 'Education cannot compensate for society, *New Society* 15, 344–347, and in Rubenstein, J. and Stoneman, B. eds (1972) *Education for Democracy*.

10. Labov, W. (1973) 'The logic of non-standard english', in Keddie, N. ed. *Tinker, Tailor . . . . . The Myth of Cultural Deprivation*, Penguin Books.

11. Bernstein, B. (1969) op. cit. [*ref. 9 above*].

12. Bernstein, B. (1969) op. cit.

13. See example, Burt, C. (1937) op. cit. [*ref. 1 above*].

14. This point is argued fully in the Plowden Report, Central Advisory Council for Education (England) (1967) *Children and their Primary Schools: A report.* H.M.S.O.

15. The Crowther Report, op. cit [*ref. 2 above*].

16. See for example; Jackson, B. and Marsden, D. (1966) op. cit. [*ref. 4 above*]; and Himmelweit, H. and Sealy, A. P. (1966) *The School as an Agent of Socialisation.*

17. Leacock, E. G. ed. (1971) *The Culture of Poverty: A Critique,* Simon and Schuster, New York.

18. An example is the Liverpool Education Priority Area Project headed by Eric Midwinter.

19. Midwinter, E. (1972) op. cit. [*ref. 24, Ch. 2*].

20. See for example, Young, M. and McGeeney, P. (1968) *Learning Begins at Home*, Routledge and Kegan Paul.

21. There are a number of social class related factors thought to have a bearing on socialisation; these are often the variables chosen for study in a particular research project, and include family size, birth order, the number and types of newspapers taken, father's job, and so on. Many of these variables are not regarded as important by educationists and sociologists as criticisms mount of the empirical methods of data collection in sociology. There is a summary of the relationship between some of these variables and socialisation in Farmer, M. (1969) op. cit. [*ref. 2 Ch. 2*] 'The prognosis of achievement', pp. 102–9

22. Flude, M. (1974) op. cit. [*ref. 7 above*].

23. Keddie, N. (1973) op. cit., p. 8 [*Ref. 10 above*].

24. Bernstein, B. (1969) 'Education cannot compensate for society', op. cit. [*ref. 9 above*].

25. Flude, M. (1974) op. cit. [*ref. 7 above*].

26. Referred to as the term coined by Wilson, T. P., in Gorbutt, D. (1972) op. cit. [*ref. 37, Ch. 2*].

27. This point is discussed elsewhere, see Pring, R. 'Knowledge out of control', *Education for Teaching,* Autumn 1972.

28. Simon, B. (1957) *Streaming and Unstreaming in the Secondary School,* Lawrence and Wishart.

29. Nash, R. (1973) op. cit. [*ref. 4, Ch. 3*].

30. Hargreaves, D. (1968) op. cit. [*ref. 12, Ch. 3*] and Lacey, C. (1970) op. cit. [*ref. 21, Ch. 2*].

31. Keddie, N. (1971) 'Classroom knowledge', in Young, M. F. D. ed., op. cit., pp. 135–56 [*ref. 4, Ch. 3*].

32. Keddie, N. (1971) op. cit.

33. Hopper, E. and Osborn, M. (1975) op. cit. [*ref. 3, Ch. 3*].

34. Young, M. F. D. (1971) in the introduction to Young, M. F. D. ed., op. cit. [*ref. 4, Ch. 3*].

35. Williamson, B. (1974) 'Continuities and discontinuities in the sociology of education', in Flude, M. and Ahier, J. eds, op. cit. [*ref. 7 above*].

36. This point has been established by school studies like those of Hargreaves and Lacey, before the explosion of popularity of the alternative paradigm approaches.

37. Jencks, C. A. (1973) *Inequality: A Reassessment of the Effect of Family and Schooling in America,* Allen Lane, London. See also, Boudon, R. (1974) *Education, Opportunity and Social Inequality; Changing Prospects in Western Society,* Wiley–Interscience, New York.

38. Most of the authors of the works referred to in this chapter

include in their analyses some suggestions for equalising educational opportunities.

Chapter 5   Adult socialisation

1. See for example Elkin, F. (1960) op. cit. [*ref. 3, Ch. 1*].

2. These areas of influence are noted in Brim, O. G. (1968) 'Adult socialisation', in Clausen, J. A. ed., op. cit. [*ref. 14, Ch. 1*].

3. See pp. 10–13.

4. Mead, G. H. (1934) op. cit. [*ref. 9, Ch. 1*].

5. Brim. O. G. (1968) op. cit. [*ref. 2 above*].

6. This is argued further in Brim, O. G. and Wheeler, S. (1966) *Socialisation After Childhood: Two Essays*, Wiley.

7. Glaser, B. and Strauss, A. (1968) *Status Passage*, Routledge and Kegan Paul.

8. Miller, A. (1967) 'After the fall', in *Collected Plays*, Secker and Warburg, London.

9. See for example, Packard, V. (1960) *The Hidden Persuaders*, Longman.

10. For a discussion of party affiliations among adolescents and how these may relate to home and school socialisation see Tapper, T. (1971) *Young People and Society*, Faber and Faber, London, Chaps. 7, 8 and 9.

11. Butler, B. and Stokes, D. (1969) *Political Change in Britain*, Macmillan.

12. Rose, R. (1970) *People in Politics*, Faber and Faber, London. In this work the author argues that the connection between social class and political party is diminishing.

13. Included among the studies of student political involvement during the 1960s are: Feuer, L. (1969) *The Conflict of Generations: the Character and Significance of student Movements*, Heinemann; Emerson, R. ed. (1968) *Students and Politics in Developing Nations*, Pall Mall Press; Blackstone, T. (1970) *Students in Conflict LSE in 1967*, LSE Research Monograph No. 5., Weidenfeld and Nicolson, London.

14. Lewis, O. (1961) *The Children of Sanchez: Autobiography of a Mexican Family*, Random House, New York.

15. Bronfenbrenner, U. (1971) *Two Worlds of Childhood; U.S. and U.S.S.R.,* Allen and Unwin; Caudill, W.R. and De Vos, G. (1956) 'Achievement, culture and personality; the case of the Japanese Americans', *American Anthropologist,* **58,** 1102–26; Mead, M. (1964) *Sex and Temperament in Three Primitive Societies;* Routledge and Kegan Paul; Caudill, W. R. and Scarr, H. A. (1962) 'Japanese value orientations and culture change', *Ethology* **1**, 53–91.

16. Figures for the United States appear in Mogey, J. (1964) 'Family and community in urban industrial societies', in Christianson,H. J. ed., *Handbook of Marriage and the Family,* Rand McNalley.

17. See for example: Board of Education (1911) *Interim Memorandum on the Teaching of Homecraft in Girls' Secondary Schools*, H.M.S.O.; and, Acland Report (1913) *Report of the Consultative Committee on Practical Work in Secondary Schools*, H.M.S.O.

18. Danziger, K. (1971) op. cit. p. 61 [*ref. 16, Ch. 1*].

19. Young, M. and Willmott, P. (1957) *Family and Kinship in East London,* Routledge and Kegan Paul, and Penguin Books (1962).

20. The mother's loss of a son from her territory, plus the replacement of her power with that of another, younger woman, constitutes a considerable drop in the well-entrenched status and behaviour patterns of maternal life. See for example, Banks, J. A. and O. (1964) *Feminism and Family Planning in Victorian England*, Liverpool University Press. In this work Mr and Mrs Banks correlate family size and female emancipation.

21. Deutscher, I. (1962) 'Socialization for post-parental life', in Rose, A. M. ed., *Human Behaviour and Social Process*, Routledge and Kegan Paul

22. See for example the study on American marriage, Blood, R. and Wolfe, D. M. (1960) *Husbands and Wives: The Dynamics of Married Living*, Free Press. There is another discussion of post-parental socialisation in Harris, C. C. (1969) *The Family*, George Allen and Unwin, Chap. 7.

23. Bernstein, B. (1969) op. cit. [*ref. 9, Ch. 4*].

24. Midwinter, E. (1972) op. cit. [*ref. 24, Ch. 2*].

25. Part of the Liverpool Education Priority Area project was concerned with educating adults. See EPA pamphlet, *Adult Education* by Tom Burns.

26. Hopper, E. and Osborn, M. (1975) op. cit. [*ref. 3 Ch. 3*].

27. A sociological analysis of such courses appears in Roberts, K., White, G. E., and Parker, H. (1973) *The Character Training Industry: Adventure Training Schemes in Britain*, David and Charles.

28. Young, M. and Willmott, P. (1957) op. cit. [*ref. 19 above*] in their study of East London suggest that the move to suburban Greenlea constitutes a form of upward mobility. Sociologists rarely dwell on problems of adjustment in downward mobility – see for example: Jackson, B. and

Marsden, D. (1966) op. cit. [*ref. 4 Ch. 4*] and Clark, B. R. (1961) 'The "Cooling-out" function in higher education', in Halsey, A. H., Floud, J. and Anderson, A. A. eds., op. cit. [*ref. 30, Ch. 3*].

29. Brim, O. G. (1968) op. cit. [*ref. , Ch.*].

30. A range of learning for immigrants is described in Eisenstadt, S. N. (1954) *The Absorption of Immigrants,* Routledge and Kegan Paul. See also: Banton, M. (1967) *Racial Minorities,* Tavistock; Baxter, P. and Sansom, B. eds (1972) *Race and Social Differences,* Penguin Books.

31. As for example in the increasing number of adult language classes and other cultural assimilation courses available in British schools.

32. See for example: Becker, H. (1963) *Outsiders: Studies in the Sociology of Deviance,* Free Press, New York; Becker, H. (1964) *The Other Side: Perspectives on Deviance,* Free Press, New York; Garfinkel, H. (1956) 'Conditions of successful degradation ceremonies', *American Journal of Sociology* 61, 420–424 Taylor, I., Walton, P. and Young, J. eds (1973) *The New Criminology,* Routledge and Kegan Paul; Taylor, I., Walton, P. and Young, J. eds (1975) *Critical Criminology,* Routledge and Kegan Paul.

33. McQuail, D. (1969) *Towards a Sociology of Mass Communication,* Collier–Macmillan.

34. For example the first public television transmissions in South Africa were received in July 1976.

35. The power of mass radio communication was dramatically illustrated in America by the hysteria following a broadcast of Orson Welles programme *The Invasion from Mars.* So realistic did this production appear to be that telephone switchboards were jammed by callers seeking further infor-

mation, and the roads leading from towns were blocked with cars and fleeing pedestrains.

36. Danziger, K. (1971) op. cit., p. 118–21 [ref.16, Ch.21].

37. Himmelweit, H. T., Oppenheim, A. N. and Vince, P. (1958) *Television and the Child,* Oxford University Press.

38. Larsen, O. N. ed. (1968) *Violence and Mass Media,* Harper and Rowe, New York.

39. This was the case in the so-called 'Clockwork Orange' murder in 1972, when an old man was beaten up and kicked to death in a carbon copy of a murder scene from the film *A Clockwork Orange* which was on general release at the time.

40. Recent examples of the effective use of mass communication to serve an immediate need in this country are the 'Save Water' advertising campaign during the summer and autumn of 1976, and the widespread publicity given to the dangers of careless use of fireworks over a period of years, mainly between 1971 and 1976, a project which apparently resulted in a significant saving of life and prevention of injury among young children.

41. Galbraith, J. K. (1967) *The New Industrial State,* Penguin Books.

42. Marcuse, H. (1964) *One Dimensional Man,* Routledge and Kegan Paul.

43. Marcuse, H. (1973) *Eros and Civilisation*, Abacus Books, p. 11

44. McQuail, D. (1969) op. cit. p. 86, [*ref. 33 above*] quoting Peterson, T. *et al,* (1965) *The Mass Media and Modern Society,* Holt, Rinehart and Winston.

45. Roberts, K. (1971) *The Sociology of Leisure,* Longman;

Burns, T. (1967) 'A meaning in everyday life', *New Society*, **25,** 243.

46. There are some indications that this is being attempted directly through advertisements, re-training programmes, the broadcast of safety standards on television, the production of industrial short films and increasingly, through popular television drama.

47. Gerth, H. H. and Mills, C. W. eds (1948) op. cit. [*ref., Ch. 3*].

48. Newcomb, T. and B. (1950) *Social Psychology,* Dryden.

49. Musgrove, F. (1970) *Patterns of Power and Authority in English Education,* Heinemann. The same point is also argued by Bernstein, B. (1969) op. cit. [ref. 9, ch. 4]

50. Levinson, D. (1973) 'Role, personality and social structure in the organisational setting', in Salaman, G. and Thompson, K. eds, *People and Organisations*, Longman, pp. 223–37.

51. Watkins, G. (1976) *Social Control,* Longman. See especially the section 'Social control in industry' in Chapter 4.

52. Such challenge has been recently exemplified during the public enquiries held into proposed motorway routes in the regions of Winchester and Derbyshire.

53. Watkins, D., (1976), op. cit. pp. 56–64. This section includes a useful discussion of the concept of legitimacy of authority in society.

Chapter 6   Conclusion

1. Giner, S. (1972) *Sociology,* Martin Robertson.

2. Peters, R. S. (1964) *Education as Initiation,* University of London.

3. Bowles, S. (1975) 'Unequal education and the reproduction of the social divison of labour', in Dale, R., Esland, G. and MacDonald, M. eds (1976) *Schooling and Capitalism:*

A Sociological Reader, Routledge and Kegan Paul and The Open University Press.

4. Patrick, J. (1972) *A Glasgow Gang Observed,* Eyre Methuen.

5. Examples of such difficulties are discussed in the following studies: Carter M. P. (1966) *Into Work,* Penguin Books; Maizels, E. J. (1971) *Adolescent Needs and the Transition From School to Work,* University of London, Athlone Press; Veness, T. (1962) op. cit. [*ref. 9 Ch. 3*]; Roberts, K. (1971) *From School to Work: A Study of the Youth Employment Service,* David and Charles.

6. See for example Douvan, E. and Adelson, J. (1966) *The Adolescent Experience,* Wiley, New York.

7. This point is made by Turner, R. H. (1964) op. cit. [*ref. 25, Ch. 3*].

8. See for example, Finlayson, D. and Cohen, L. (1967) 'The teacher's role: a comparative study of the conceptions of college of education students and head teachers', *British Journal of Educational Psychology,* 37, pp. 22–31.

9. Roberts, K., White, G. E. and Parker, H. J., (1973) op. cit. [*ref. 27, Ch. 5*].

10. Musgrove, F. (1964) *Youth and the Social Order,* Routledge and Kegan Paul. Musgrove argues that the older generation fail to recognise the conforming qualities of the adolescent in order to persist with repressive practices on grounds of altruism.

11. Parker, H. J. (1974) *View From the Boys,* David and Charles is an example of a study which points out this trend.

12. This point is fully discussed in respect of education in the paper by Hextall, I. and Sarup, M. 'Who Knows? School knowledge, evaluation and alienation', B.S.A. paper, March 1975

143

13. Possibly this might be more accurately called praxis rather than creativity. Praxis is that type of activity which fully characterises its producer, and is understood as having an intrinsic meaning, rather than meaning derived from its 'cause', in the sense which traditional scientific analysis interprets cause and effect. The idea of praxis to be developed in students is not the aim of most school curricula in this country.

14. Bernstein, B. (1969) op. cit. [ref. 9, ch. 4].

15. Keddie, N. (1971) op. cit. [*ref. 31, Ch. 4*].

Index

Index